Praise for *Once Up*

"Bellebuono's deep curiosity and passion for exploring the role of the healer throughout time and around the world has resulted in this mystical and marvelous collection of stories, myth, and fairy tale insights that challenge us on the seeker's journey."

—**CAROL BEDROSIAN**, publisher of *Spirit of Change Magazine*

"An elaborate and refreshing revisitation of ancient stories as well as modern ones. Holly draws from nearly every cultural myth and legend. From Gilgamesh to Alice in Wonderland, Baba Yaga, Star Wars, Harry Potter, and many others. This study offers a categorical dissection and definition of the various symbols encountered in tales about journeying from curiosity, facing fear and that experience leading to learned wisdom and transcendence. I truly enjoyed this read."

—**LATA CHETTRI-KENNEDY**, founder of Flower Power Herbs and Roots, Inc. (FlowerPower.net)

"Informed by a plethora of narratives from ancient mythology to modern film, from fairy tales to contemporary children's books, from fantasy to coming-of-age stories, award-winning author, herbalist, and international speaker Holly Bellebuono identifies five specific locations pivotal to the hero's or heroine's quest and explores their symbolic meanings against the backdrop of World Journeys. *Once Upon a Place* offers intriguing insights into the significance of the Cavern, the Deep, the Vessel, the Forest, and the Labyrinth as symbolic spaces for personal challenge and transformation. Eloquently written, this book is bound to appeal to a wide range of audiences and should be a must for any college library."

—**SUSANNE EVEN**, PhD, professor of German at Indiana University and co-editor of *SCENARIO* Journal

"*Once Upon a Place* captures the magic elements shared in ancient myths and fairy tales as well as in modern stories told on 'the big screen.' As an exhibitor of films, I seek to provide audiences with the context they need to view, appreciate, and enjoy films and to learn from them to enhance their human experience. Bellebuono's book provides this context with great insights into

story-craft, symbolism and imagery, especially what she identifies as the five locations of the hero's journey. It's a book for every aspiring writer and film enthusiast."
—**RICHARD PARADISE**, founder of Martha's Vineyard Film Society

"Well-known herbalist, writer, teacher, coach, and wise woman Holly Bellebuono explores the magical imagery of folk story and myth in her new book *Once Upon a Place*. Two ideas featured at the heart of this book are at the core of all quest stories: the Abyss and the World Journey. For women searching to gain knowledge and growth, this book explores these myths in a way that is personal, transformative, and genuine. Recommended."
—**ANNE NEWKIRK NIVEN**, editor and publisher of *SageWoman* magazine

"Bellebuono uses the concept of the World Journey to present classic themes and topics of self-discovery in a new light. Through the timeless avenue of story, readers can explore the significance of location and the transformative power each setting holds. Whether revisiting familiar tales or discovering new ones, a hands-on discussion guide helps readers put into practice the wisdom learned along the way. A truly transcendent experience!"
—**EMBER GRANT**, author of *Mythology for a Magical Life*

ONCE
UPON
A PLACE

ONCE UPON A PLACE

Forests, Caverns & Other
Places of Transformation in
Myths, Fairy Tales & Film

HOLLY BELLEBUONO

Foreword by Jack Zipes

LLEWELLYN
WOODBURY, MINNESOTA

FIRST EDITION
First Printing, 2025

Book design by Christine Ha
Cover design by Kevin R. Brown
Interior illustrations by Sveta Dorosheva

Llewellyn Publications is a registered trademark of Llewellyn Worldwide Ltd.

Library of Congress Cataloging-in-Publication Data (Pending)
ISBN: 978-0-7387-7937-9

Llewellyn Worldwide Ltd. does not participate in, endorse, or have any authority or responsibility concerning private business transactions between our authors and the public.

All mail addressed to the author is forwarded but the publisher cannot, unless specifically instructed by the author, give out an address or phone number.

Any internet references contained in this work are current at publication time, but the publisher cannot guarantee that a specific location will continue to be maintained. Please refer to the publisher's website for links to authors' websites and other sources.

Llewellyn Publications
A Division of Llewellyn Worldwide Ltd.
2143 Wooddale Drive
Woodbury, MN 55125-2989
www.llewellyn.com

Printed in the United States of America

Other Books by Holly Bellebuono

Llewellyn's Little Book of Herbs

*An Herbalist's Guide to Formulary: The Art &
Science of Creating Effective Herbal Remedies*

*The Healing Kitchen: Cooking with Nourishing
Herbs for Health, Wellness, and Vitality*

*Women Healers of the World: The Traditions,
History, and Geography of Herbal Medicine*

A Goal-Setting Guide for Open-Minded Business Owners

*The Authentic Herbal Healer: The Complete Guide to Herbal
Formulary & Plant-Inspired Medicine for Every Body System*

*The Essential Herbal for Natural Health: How to Transform
Easy-to-Find Herbs into Healing Remedies for the Whole Family*

How to Use Herbs for Natural Health

For my love, David.

Acknowledgments

Many thanks go to my friends and family who have patiently read this book as it was conceived many years ago. I'd like to thank Tom Owens and Keya Guimaraes for providing their editorial guidance as the manuscript went through its many phases.

I'd like to express my appreciation to my agent, Jody Kahn, for her unflagging support through the development process as I explored ideas and formats.

Finally, my beloved partner, David Vigneault, deserves my unwavering gratitude for his support and belief in me.

Contents

Contents

Story Adaptations from Around the World

THE CAVERN
Inanna (Akkad/Sumer)
Persephone (Greece)

THE DEEP
Tiamat (Ancient Babylon)
Baldr (Ancient Norse)
Gilgamesh (Ancient Sumer)

THE VESSEL
Cerridwen (Ireland)
Madchen (Germany)
Fionn (Wales)

THE FOREST
The Bear Prince (Switzerland)
Vasalisa (Russia)
Misiti and the Lion's Whisker (Ethiopia)

THE LABYRINTH

Theseus and the Minotaur (Greece)
Alice and the Caterpillar (Britain)
Spider Grandmother (Muscogee, Kiowa, and Cherokee)

FAILURE AND SUCCESS ON THE WORLD JOURNEY

Owen and the Slumber King (Wales)

FOREWORD

Exploring the Deep Meaning of Storytelling

Holly Bellebuono's remarkable book *Once Upon a Place* rediscovers the essence of myths, fairy tales, and films by connecting them to our basic wishes, needs, and struggles. Dismissing the sugary or pessimistic notions about these stories, Bellebuono takes us on several fascinating journeys to places such as the Cavern, the Abyss, the Vessel, the Forest, and the Labyrinth so that we see just how we can resolve dilemmas that prevent us from transforming ourselves into human beings with integrity. In this regard, we all identify or want to identify with the protagonists of the stories who act heroically.

Her book covers numerous narratives, from the ancient period to the present and from numerous cultures, to demonstrate how we humans are more closely related than we realize. Throughout the world, we are drawn to and enchanted by the metaphoric language of tales that stick to us like memes embedded in our brains and imagination. The narratives in her book are chosen mainly from the oral tradition because these are eternal stories. They stay with us because of their wisdom and warnings.

Bellebuono retells fifteen tales from ancient Greece, Wales, Germany, Norway, Africa, England, and more. At the end of each tale, she offers interpretations that show how closely the incidents are to those in modern times. Her insights are often psychological, including metaphorical explanations and revealing how closely human beings are to one another. As she argues, storytelling is part of our humanity and our communities.

At the end of her book, she includes a resource section filled with questions and answers that might help readers explore the ideas and concepts within the tales that she has discussed. Her book is not just a work to read and enjoy but one to act upon in our daily lives. In short, Holly Bellebuono's book is a *real* adventure, which offers hope that storytelling can do more than amuse us—that it can also indicate ways to live with compassion and courage.

—Jack Zipes

INTRODUCTION

There's More to the Story Than You Know: Myth, Fairy Tale, and Film

In 1865 a math teacher named Charles Dodgson took on the pen name Lewis Carroll to write the tale *Alice's Adventures in Wonderland*. Five years later, he produced its sequel, *Through the Looking-Glass, and What Alice Found There*. In these bright, mesmerizing, yet somehow sinister stories, he created a beastly queen, strange animals, and magical portals through which young Alice traveled to meet a changed version of herself. At first, Alice was alarmed at seeing a white rabbit rush past her, taking a watch out of its pocket and popping down a hole under a hedge, but then "in another moment down went Alice after it," Lewis Carroll tells us, "never once considering how in the world she was to get out again."[1]

How in the world indeed. To go down, as we shall see, is the most natural thing, but to get back up again—that is the surprisingly profound achievement upon which this book is based.

Roughly thirty years after Carroll published *Alice*, L. Frank Baum published *The Wonderful Wizard of Oz*, introducing what would become two

---

1. Carroll, *Alice's Adventures in Wonderland; Through the Looking Glass; What Alice Found There; The Hunting of the Snark*, 10.

1

of the world's most famous witches and having his characters travel to key memorable places that influenced the progress of their entire story: a meandering path through a dark forest and a cacophony of buildings in the Emerald City, a land of checkerboards, and a garden of giant mushrooms. Alice travels through portals into labyrinths of changing dimensions, and Dorothy wanders through woodlands pierced by the shrieks of flying monkeys.

These dizzying locations are not just an add-on or a second thought; they are, as we will see, an integral and core part of the Journey. Storytellers long ago crafted these locations intentionally to support the hero's quest for enlightenment. In this book, we'll identify and examine the five key locations that exist in many of the World Journey stories we've inherited from cultures around the globe, exploring how each location positions the seeker for growth in a hostile, bewildering, or magical place. But first, let's define two key parts of our exploration: the Abyss and the World Journey.

The Ancient Abyss and the World Journey

Two ideas feature at the heart of this book and at the core of all quest stories: they are the Abyss and the World Journey.

The Abyss is one of humanity's oldest and most tenacious ideas that has been used for millennia to describe a place that is deep, inaccessible, extremely dangerous, and somehow at the core of understanding. In some ancient texts, it is synonymous with the deep ocean and is often portrayed as the sea in films today. But its broader meaning encompasses *all* the dark, deep places we go when we embark on an adventure to find answers. It's where the obstacles lie and the challenges are found, often in the form of a beast or monster that must be overcome. The Abyss is arguably the most meaningful concept in our collection of stories because it shapes the idea of what a challenge means.

The World Journey is a much newer term, which I've adapted from Joseph Campbell's Hero's Journey. You may be familiar with the storyline, or plot, of the Hero's Journey, as it was coined by the Sarah Lawrence College professor of literature in the twentieth century. In it, the hero goes through a sequence of experiences designed to help them face and overcome the many challenges of life, often in the context of a quest or adventure. Campbell presented a structure for this process, and it has become a reliable plot outline for the stages of character development in many modern films and stories, such as J. R. R. Tolkein's *The Lord of the Rings* or George Lucas's *Star Wars*. Campbell's process leads toward self-actualization with deliberate stages that create a plot, which leads a man, and seldom a woman, through each step in specific order to experience certain hardships and, ultimately, achieve epiphany or personal growth.

But there's more to a story than the plot. Whereas Campbell taught the steps of the transformative process, in this book we'll explore *where* it happens, which just as powerfully influences the outcome of the story as the steps or the process. The *where* enriches the *how*, making quest stories deeper and more meaningful. These colorful and fascinating locations are a core part of the adventure, influencing how the seeker faces challenges before they rise up and resurrect.

The plotlines of the fictional Alice and Dorothy, for instance, have both young girls facing adolescence and meeting fearsome beasts. But to do so, they must leave one place and enter another—a *location*—that is the epicenter of their experience and influences every decision they make. They leave their homes and enter another realm or world, which serves as an inspiring metaphor and gives the story shape. The World Journey uses these metaphors to refer to the roads within that must be traveled, the inward journey that takes us *elsewhere*.

In other words, the Abyss is where the adventure of the World Journey happens, and in this book, we will identify and celebrate five specific locations nearly all quest stories are based upon, which are integral to the imagery and success of a hero's adventure.

The Locations of the World Journey

The locations of the World Journey appear widely in all cultures around the world; they are present in fairy tales, myths, legends, and screenplays from around the globe. These five key locations are as follows:

1. **The Cavern:** This can be portrayed as a cave, tunnel, vast cavern, or simply a hole in the ground that serves as a portal to the Underworld. It's an earthy, chthonic image and examples range

from Hell and Hades to Jules Verne's fantastical realm in the center of the earth.

2. **The Deep:** This is the vast ocean, so deep and massive it seems to be without boundaries. Heroes plunge down into the ocean on their quests, or they or their funeral barges sail across its surface.

3. **The Vessel:** The Vessel contains water, but it is smaller than the ocean with a more familiar shape. The Vessel can be a bowl, cauldron, chalice, or even a small well, and it often possesses magical healing qualities or the ability to renew life.

4. **The Forest:** Many children's fairy tales begin with a hero going "into the woods," the tangled, dark, and mysterious Forest where the adventure happens. This location is associated with trees, which, as we'll see, combine their mystical powers of uniting the upper- and underworlds to bring their own magic to a seeker's adventure.

5. **The Labyrinth:** This is a mazelike structure within which a seeker travels, often turning and twisting back on their path to find their way through. Many Labyrinth stories feature thread, yarn, or spider's silk with which the seeker finds their way back out.

These locations range from underground to underwater to woodlands to outer space and even through time itself, and each place influences the progress of the story. In this book, we'll explore the colors, images, and shapes in these very different locations and ask how they affect what the character does. How does the seeker act because they've entered a particular location of the Journey? How do the heroes work their way through these locations to find enlightenment on the other side?

Characters will experience enlightenment differently depending on their location in the Abyss. For example, in the Welsh story of Fionn, the boy's experience sticking his fingers into the brew of a magic cauldron (the Vessel) is more domestic than Theseus's adventure twisting round the royal maze of the Greek Labyrinth, yet they both experience transformation and become heroes in their cultures. Gretel's heroism fighting the Witch in the Forest is much different from the goddess Inanna passing through the gates to the Underworld, yet both achieve enlightenment and return to their homes wiser and stronger. In Hans Christian Andersen's *The Little Mermaid*, Ariel's quest through the watery Deep is vastly different from Joseph Cooper's time-bending trip through the Labyrinth of space in *Interstellar*, yet they each achieve awareness and insight that satisfies their life purpose. Critically, they all experience symbolic Descent and Resurrection, going into a difficult place and emerging stronger, which is the point of World Journey stories. We'll explore these and other stories and films to discover how the five mythic locations enrich the story.

Today's Adventure Stories

The Abyss and the World Journey—where the heroes go and what they experience—embody the very nature of human change, though many stories can be overlooked as simple child's play, especially when it comes to fairy tales. Heroic knights fighting dragons or a girl carrying a basket to her grandmother? Many could dismiss these as bedtime tales. But while these stories may seem soft, they likely began as images directed squarely at those about to experience a profound life change such as puberty. These tales and their enchanting symbols have influenced not only our idea of what a hero's adventure should be but of what success looks like and how personal achievement is earned.

Originally etched into stone slabs and scribbled on papyrus, many of these stories and fairy tales have become Disney blockbusters, printed bestsellers, and on-screen hits. The symbol of the Abyss perennially renews itself, showing up at movie theaters every month with its deep-rooted ideas of Descent and Resurrection, and films inspired by the World Journey, such as *O Brother, Where Art Thou?* and *Jurassic Park*, are enjoyed by people of all ages.

Why do they endure? Why are World Journey stories some of the most popular stories shared again and again in cultures around the world? Because we can relate to a situation where a person falls (or is pushed) into a terrifying cave and must survive. We understand what it means to find oneself in a frightening "wilderness" with no support, no skills, no training, no hand to hold. We've been there ourselves through adversities, such as the loss of a loved one, being the new kid at school, or failing in a business or relationship, or through experiences as simple as missing a chance, forgetting an idea, or failing to live up to our own (or others') expectations.

Today's audiences love the same images that captivated people hundreds of years ago: water, darkness, dragons, beasts, labyrinths, forests, and caverns. These symbols endure because they don't speak about money or politics. They don't appeal to our wallets or even, in a direct sense, to our minds. Instead, they speak to our innermost fears and desires, to the obstacles we all face and the meaningful purpose we feel when we overcome them.

The story of a person who falls into the Abyss and is never seen again is not an inspiring story. It teaches nothing except to watch where you walk. But the story of a woman who braves the face of a lion to pluck its whisker, or of a man who desperately crosses the Deep in a small boat to find answers, or of a scientist who plumbs the ocean's depths in search of meaning and returns home as a much stronger person—that is an intriguing story and one that implies self-fulfillment and maturity.

In other words, Newton's gravitational notion of "what goes up must come down" is not nearly as old or as relevant as "what goes *down* must come *up*." Such a story inspires and motivates, and it even implies heroism, which is what most of these stories are mistaken for on the surface (and how Campbell named them). But the reason these stories have survived centuries, and in some cases millennia, is not because they celebrate heroism but because they teach that these traits of survival and fulfillment are attainable for *everyone*, even the most mortal of us. Even the silliest, poorest, most confused, and frightened of us can make changes in our lives to experience not only enlightenment but epiphany. Recognizing this when we have screens in every room, distractions at every turn, and challenges in every aspect of our lives is essential; the quest is not only for the hero, but it is for each of us.

The Value of a Challenge

Adversity, hardship, and conflict are not concepts we are naturally drawn to. Parents and caregivers generally try to shield their children from hardship in an attempt to protect them from the hurtful obstacles of life and keep them safe. But the process of maturing means facing difficulties head-on rather than avoiding them. While it includes terrible challenges, the purpose of the

World Journey is not to scare or punish us but rather to support our growth, and to grow, we must look in the face of that which frightens us the most.

Unfortunately, many of today's stories of princesses and dragons are sugary and fluffy, diluted shades of what used to be quite powerful symbols. Modern adaptations of fairy tales would have us believe that success is easy—that if we only wish upon a star or wrinkle our noses our dreams will come true. The original versions, however, showed that change is far more difficult. Original fairy tales guide us down darker paths with frightening beasts and scary forests that no seeker truly wants to walk into. And I would argue that while those original stories, especially those collected and recorded hundreds of years ago by Charles Perrault and the Grimm brothers, were indeed dark, frightening, and often overtly violent or callous, they should not be sugared over simply because they are scary, depressing, or harsh. They served a much-needed purpose by symbolically painting a reality that most people experienced and still do experience in their lives: namely, challenging situations that push us to our limits and are, in fact, our very best opportunities for change and growth. Those storytellers and parents long ago knew that persistence allows us to become strong and resilient adults. They knew that facing our fears can make us compassionate, forgiving, and joyful, and that making difficult decisions instills in us a feeling of accomplishment and maturity. From their stories, we learn that experiences of confusion and uncertainty can open our minds to new ideas and creative expression that allow us as individuals and as societies to flourish.

World Journey stories teach us to overcome adversity, but more importantly, they teach us how to *experience* adversity in the first place. Successful myths, religious texts, and fairy tales—and modern screenplays and films— do not skirt the issue of hardship and conflict, nor do they encourage us to finish the hard work as quickly as possible. The characters in J. K. Rowling's *Harry Potter* do not face obstacles and beasts simply to advance the plot but to develop the inner courage and tenacity needed to grow as individuals within society. Mythic stories put us squarely in the middle of the hardest tasks we can imagine, and they force us to work hard, to guess, to take leaps of faith, and to push ourselves to the limit.

They also teach us that it's worth it to "dive deep" and to experience a change so drastic that it is profound. In fact, though they seem superficial now in the age of animated princesses, the early stories of Little Red Riding Hood and Snow White are popular precisely because they show these challenges, as do the Bible story of Jonah and the Mesopotamian poem of Gilgamesh, which is perhaps the oldest story we've ever found. Created more than four thousand years ago, Gilgamesh was an amazingly influential and well-loved character whose journey taught scores of generations of children the meaning of perseverance, curiosity, and spiritual growth. As we'll see in chapter 5, his tale depicts a hero in terribly dire circumstances who does not shrug off hardship but instead plows right through it, diving deep (literally and symbolically) to work through his fear of death. Only after completing difficult tasks and overcoming obstacles does he mature as a person. Of course, he fails to find immortality, but that's the point.

Imagery: The Role of Symbols in Storycraft

Symbols and metaphors are more than enchanting pieces of literature. They are suggestive in such a way that makes them very useful in stories that aim to teach something. One reason these stories have been popular for generations is because they don't come right out and say, "Things will get much harder before they get better." Instead, they use symbols, colorful imagery, and adventures that speak to us in ways that literal statements never can. The human mind often avoids that which appears dangerous or hard, but cloaking a lesson in symbolic imagery can make learning easier.

Images are like pictures in the mind's eye, and stories, of course, show a thousand pictures. A child may not remember facts and figures but will breathlessly wait to find out what happens to Beowulf after he plunges into the deep water to attack Grendel the dragon—especially when Beowulf drops his slippery sword right onto the bottom of the dragon's lair. Or what happens to little girl Vasalisa when she is sent out to walk into the dark forest to the witch's hut to ask for coal for her family's fire. In the woods, she hears whispering voices and feels the cloaks of mysterious riders galloping by her on horseback, and then she faces the frightening witch who wants to eat her. Oh no! How could it get worse? But it does, and children hang on to every word, perhaps only much later realizing they were listening to an ancient collection of lessons that teach resilience, tenacity, and belief in oneself.

This is where metaphor and imagery work their magic. Through the symbols of story, especially of the beastly wolf, witch, or whale, these lessons are learned. Through symbols, we know that the lead character in the story is not living a literal experience but undergoing something figurative that is much more meaningful than what the surface story indicates. For instance, seeing Eve beside a tree talking with a snake is, on a literal level, a fascinating conversation between a human and a reptile; on a symbolic level, it is indicative of great personal growth and the search for immortality as envisioned by our ancestors. These symbols either began as metaphors or later came to symbolize certain qualities and characteristics of the human quest for growth. In this book, we will recognize these and other symbols in stories as more than convenient plot points.

Navigating the Locations of the Journey

Not every story, of course, is a World Journey story. Many myths are solely creation or origin stories, which explain how animals got their fur or how the moon was placed into the sky. Many children's tales are merely morality or etiquette lessons, especially such classics as Aesop's fables. But so many stories center on *the quest, the adventure,* or *the journey* that I endeavored to scour literature and read myths and fairy tales with fresh eyes to find clues of transformation and the use of specific locations of the World Journey—attempts by someone in the past to reach forward with comforting words of encouragement through symbolic storycraft.

In addition to encouragement, I think the storytellers were using symbolic imagery, especially the five locations, to teach us not only how to experience but how to *navigate* the path forward. Descending into a cavern or the ocean or entering a confusing labyrinth requires the skills of navigation (to get out) and negotiation (to leave with what you came for).

The 2012 Ang Lee film *The Life of Pi* is a good example. When I sat down to watch the film, I, like millions of others, was caught up in the breathless adventure and terrifying circumstance of a boy who survives the sinking of a ship in the middle of the Pacific. Alone and frightened, Pi Patel manages to overcome hunger, danger, loneliness, and fear all while sailing across the vast, empty ocean. He faces unique challenges that make his story memorable, but certain imagery makes it clear that this story's backbone is the location of the Deep; he floats across a seemingly boundaryless ocean, faces a terrifying beast, is nearly eaten by a carnivorous monster, suffers thirst and sunburn, and spends weeks, if not months, stranded and isolated in a watery place without form, shape, direction, or horizon. If his story was set in another location, such as a cavern, his lessons would be very different, though ultimately overcoming adversity and rising to become his higher Self would be the end result. The boy learns not only to navigate his way across the surface of the Deep but also how to navigate his way through grief, fear, panic, and heartbreak.

Each of these five locations is a symbol creatively and intentionally used in World Journey literature, and we'll explore them all here, in stories ranging from the Native American tale of Spider Grandmother to the Greek myth of Persephone to the European fairy tales recorded by the Grimm brothers to the adventures of Frodo Baggins to interstellar cinematic voyages through space and time. In fact, we'll celebrate stories from fifteen cultures, both ancient and modern, including tales from ancient Mesopotamia (Babylon and Sumer), Ethiopia, Greece, Ireland, Norway, North America, Russia, and Wales. It is important to me to be as inclusive as possible of multiple cultures and traditions, because when researching myths and tales, it is easy to focus on ancient Greek myths, for instance, which are plentiful. Instead, we'll touch on some of the lesser-known quest stories that feature the five locations of the World Journey and that celebrate positive transformation, as well as explore modern films as they capture the World Journey on the big screen.

How to Use This Book

Here, we will unpack popular stories to find out what makes them the most inspirational and relevant tales ever told, especially looking at one of the most influential parts of the story: *where* it happens.

First, in part I, we will introduce three of the most essential concepts of the World Journey. These concepts are at the core of every personal transformation journey, and we can't get far without exploring them. They are:

1. **Descent and Resurrection:** These refer to the actual (or symbolic) act of going down and coming back up. We'll explore

why humanity thinks of adventure in these terms and why quest stories make use of these concepts.

2. **Chaos and Void:** These states of mind often mirror our environment, and characters generally face one or the other—or both—in their attempts to gain clarity and direction. We'll explore why these concepts are needed in a story and in life and even how Chaos and Void can lead to higher consciousness and epiphany.

3. **The Beast and the Guide:** Every World Journey story pits its hero against a Beast. Here, we'll identify three of the world's most popular beasts and how they elicit strength and courage from the hero. We'll also examine the twin persona of the Guide, the (usually helpful) assistant who shows up to give the hero a helping hand.

In part II, we'll dive deep into the five intriguing locations of the World Journey: the Cavern, the Deep, the Vessel, the Forest, and the Labyrinth. In each chapter, we will identify tales and films that embody the spirit of the location and also enjoy adaptations of stories from cultures around the world. Look for these adaptations as they will be in italics and titled "A Story." Our explorations of imagery will help us determine why these special locations uniquely position seekers to overcome the greatest challenges of the human imagination.

A Note about Terminology

I find it helpful to use the term *World Journey* to reflect the philosophies of Campbell while recognizing women's role as "heroines" in their own journeys. Campbell's essays and lectures were a beacon of inspiration and understanding for many people for whom symbolism and the interconnectedness of culture were eye-opening. But he related a man's journey. He wrote that "woman…represents the totality of what can be known. The hero is the one who comes to know."[2] While this is romantic, it leaves me feeling hungry for more examples of the heroine's true experience.

---

2. Osbon, *Reflections on the Art of Living*, 223.

Today's girls have role models who are scientists, engineers, inventors, instructors, leaders, and visionaries, and girls can decide whether to marry or not (in most countries); a girl's path is not bound to her fate as a wife, as was depicted repeatedly in fairy tales in centuries past. For this reason, I've used the term *World Journey* rather than *Hero's Journey* to encompass a wider experience, and while we'll use both the words *hero* and *heroine*, we'll also use terms that apply widely, such as *seeker*, as this book is a celebration of everyone's search for truth and of both the individual and the collective pursuit of wisdom.

All Are Welcome

Additionally, it's important to recognize that exploring and understanding these concepts is not only for the experts. In fact, it's for every person to engage in these questions and to open their minds to the possibilities that exist within human nature and within the Self, to explore stories and symbols and push into growth. I will readily admit that I am neither a professional researcher nor a historian; rather, for me this book is a labor of love as much as a personal type of quest, one of learning as much as I can about the world around me. I come to the project with an herbalist's perspective, being intrigued with plants and soil and caves and stories of seeds and myths (and I take sole responsibility for any errors). Curiosity is what drives human transformation, and I invite us all to be curious.

To this end—to be open and willing to see the metaphor in these stories as chances for personal growth—please take the opportunity for further exploration by using the questions you'll find at the end of this book. These questions are included for individuals or book groups, or friends sitting to enjoy a cup of tea on the couch, to guide you on a more personal path and allow you the safe and welcoming opportunity to learn more about yourself. Where are you in your journey? What obstacles have you faced? Who is guiding you and how are you guiding others? Can you relate to these images and metaphors even though they come to us through time and distance? These questions are meant as starting points for those who are eager to relate to the world's quest imagery in their own lives, taking the symbols of story-craft and digging deeper into reflections of self-growth, core purpose, and even epiphany.

PART I
THE THREE CORE CONCEPTS ESSENTIAL TO EVERY JOURNEY

Let's start by exploring three concepts that are essential to every World Journey story. Each is an extreme, a concept of duality or danger that must be understood in every location of the Journey, no matter what the circumstance or challenge. Without these dual ideas, transformation would never occur and the story (and the seeker) would be lost. These dual concepts are: Descent and Resurrection, Chaos and Void, and the Beast and the Guide.

CHAPTER 1

Descent and Resurrection

Descent and Resurrection. Falling down and coming up. Plummeting and ascending. These are the pivotal points of the World Journey, the framework in which the seeker struggles. Aside from a culture's creation story, the idea of Descent and Resurrection is one of the oldest plotlines we've ever read. Anchored in our myths, texts, and tales, the World Journey provides the mind a way to envision entering these underworld places, and then it provides a way to imagine climbing out. Ascending. Resurrecting.

In this chapter, we'll explore the reasons that a character in a story might make a descent into a treacherous place. Perhaps surprisingly, there are several reasons that will coerce an otherwise reasonable human to enter the terrifying, dark, and dangerous Void. The reason is called a trigger, something physical or emotional that prompts a person to seek something more.

Reasons for the Descent

The trigger is something that pushes the person from a normal daily routine into something transformative and unique. Perhaps the person is experiencing boredom or complacency in normal life and needs a challenge to grow.

Or maybe he or she feels the mortal fear of death and needs to face the feelings of panic and confusion. Or the person has just begun to question his or her purpose in life and to wonder if existence has any meaning. These people may voluntarily leap into the Abyss to jump-start their own growth. But in some stories, the individual is violently forced by someone else to leave their current life—they may be pushed into a well or off a cliff or down the stairs into the dark mystery below.

Regardless of the trigger, the story indicates that the time has come for growth. In fairy tales, this often happens when the girl is facing puberty or marriage and her "evil" stepmother pushes her toward maturity. The stepmother's push is the trigger, and instead of being the punisher, she is the enabler—forcing a reluctant or frightened girl to face her future and grow up. Regardless of whether it is voluntary or not, the trigger initiates the World Journey, and if it weren't for this trigger—a thought, a feeling, or the forceful push from another person—the Descent into the Abyss would not happen and personal growth would be stunted.

Often this trigger is a rather specific event, though in some ancient stories the reference to that event has been lost. For example, in the myth of Inanna/Ishtar, the goddess Inanna voluntarily enters the Underworld, supposedly to visit her sister Ereshkigal, queen of the dead. There is no reason given for why Inanna wishes to enter other than to visit her sister, but she insists on gaining entry, hammering on the gate and shouting to be let in. There could be any number of triggers leading to Inanna wanting to enter the Land of the Dead; it may be a veiled reference to her own death, because to enter the Underworld implies death, and no one, not even a goddess, emerges from death. It could also be that Inanna wants to challenge her sister, implying that she is challenging death itself or seeking immortality, a common trigger in ancient stories such as Gilgamesh. The wish to live forever is palpable, and while gods possess immortality, humans do not, making us keen to see how it plays out for Inanna and how we might be able to cheat death ourselves using her strategy. Did Inanna make the sudden decision to "visit" the Underworld? Or did she die? Or was it a journey to discover the inner workings of the Underworld and thus cheat death?

Though the explanatory part of this myth is lost to us, other myths, religious texts, and fairy tales show us three very common triggers: (1) the appearance of puberty, which cannot be avoided, or the desire to experience maturity, (2) the desire to be a hero in the eyes of others, and (3) the pursuit of knowledge.

Trigger #1: Puberty or the Desire to Mature

Puberty is cataclysmic. It is the death of the child and the birth of an adult (presumably) ready to marry and procreate. Myths and stories probably put more energy into helping children through puberty and marriage than into any other outcome—and for good reason, as raising a healthy new member of society, where people are interdependent, is crucial. Maturity, in most cultures, is absolutely required.

The trigger for puberty and marriage can be violent—much more than simply the natural appearance of body hair or menstruation. The Greek myth of Persephone tells of the young girl Kore (*kore* is Greek for girl) playing in a meadow of flowers. Suddenly a giant hole opens beneath her, and she tumbles into a cavern. As she falls, Hades, Lord of the Dead, rushes up to her in a chariot and grabs her, pulling her downward with him. This is the beginning of the girl's descent into the Cavern, and it is entirely involuntary. Given that she is a young teen (telltale clues throughout the story hint at her physical immaturity), we can assume this is a World Journey story about progressing from an innocent child to a sexual woman. Her descent came upon her quickly and unlooked-for, and it ripped an innocent girl from her mother and replaced the girl with a woman (and now a wife) possessing the knowledge of both sex and death.

But sometimes the seeker is ready to experience maturity and simply needs the opportunity. He or she has the *desire* to grow and mature. While Kore fell into the Cavern simply because it was her time according to nature, Madchen, from the German folktale, jumped willingly into the wishing well because she was emotionally ready to transform from a girl under the constant stare of her stepmother into a (relatively) independent woman. In this tale, we watch as Madchen drops her spindle into the deep well. Whether or not she drops it on purpose remains a mystery, but the end result is clear. When her stepmother tells her to jump in and retrieve it, Madchen doesn't hesitate. She is ready to escape the confines of childhood domesticity and, with sad irony, enter the confines of wifely domesticity. (As we'll explore in chapter 6, Madchen's trials in the Abyss—like those of most girls featured in fairy tales—are to prove she is ready for adulthood by demonstrating abilities with household chores such as cleaning and cooking.)

Trigger #2: The Pursuit of Heroism

Who wants to be a hero? Apparently many people do, and it's been the basis of countless stories and tales that teach morality, courage, and maturity. With overlapping themes of boyhood-manhood rites of passage, heroism has long been a reason for embarking on the World Journey. Occasionally people want to be recognized for their heroic deeds, such as Beowulf, especially if the overt reason for entering the Abyss is to rescue someone who has been taken there (i.e., who has died and entered the Land of the Dead). Pursuing that person and stealing life from the jaws of death is a central theme of these stories—the hero pursues immortality when he fights death and wins, and immortality is no small prize. It is implicit in many of these stories, even when lasting immortal life is not the point. More often than not, a "new" life, or a new chance at life, is what the hero experiences as a result of his actions, implying that the wisdom gained to recreate the Self is as valuable as the imagined prize of actually living forever.

We find stories of descent with the intent to rescue everywhere. In Greek tales, Orpheus enters the Underworld to rescue Euridice; Dionysus descends to the Underworld to bring back his mother, Semele; and Heracles descends into the Underworld to rescue Theseus. In addition to attempts to rescue, other tales of heroism include Latin America's Obatala, who descends and is resurrected on the third day; a Hindu myth that tells of Yudhisthira descending into the Underworld, called Naraka; and the Welsh Mabinogion, the earliest discovered literature of Britain, which describes Pwyll descending to Annwn, which literally meant "very deep" and was an "otherworld."

Using the trigger of needing to rescue someone or be a hero is even seen in our modern films. George Bailey, for instance, in *It's a Wonderful Life*, a beloved Christmas tale, stands on a bridge on a freezing night desolate and depressed…but he won't jump into the river until triggered by the need to rescue Clarence, who jumps in first. As soon as George hits the water, his journey begins.

Trigger #3: The Pursuit of Knowledge

Finally, beyond coming of age or the pursuit of heroism, others descend into the liminal realm of the Underworld to learn something profound—to achieve a certain *understanding* of death and the afterlife, even if they cannot achieve immortality itself. Odysseus didn't necessarily want to live forever—but he had questions. He wanted answers about what happens after death, though Gilgamesh wanted to learn how to avert death altogether. To Odysseus, awareness and understanding were fulfilling.

The Norse god Odin descends to the land of the dead and holds a wonderful conversation with the prophetess of death, asking questions about the fate of his loved ones. Once he returns, he brings with him this new, satisfying knowledge and uses it to move forward with his life.[3]

The quest for knowledge can result from a genuine curiosity about the greatest mysteries of life and death. Ian Baker's memoir, *The Heart of the World*, about seeking and finding Shangri-La, the legendary lost valley of Tibet, describes his lifelong fascination with the lore of a hidden paradise on earth. He describes Tibetan Buddhist beliefs in *beyul*, or hidden lands, incredibly remote, secret, and isolated hidden sanctuaries where the lucky few who enter are rewarded with eye-opening insights. The more remote and inaccessible the beyul, Tibetan lore tells us, the greater the illumination to be had. Baker's teacher Sonam describes beyul as the overlap of the physical and spiritual worlds, where plants and animals have miraculous powers, where no one ages and enlightenment is found. Tantric yogis make pilgrimages to find the beyul, and men travel through treacherous places in a quest to find these hidden lands. But if the heart is not pure, the hidden lands remain shrouded, and generations of people can spend lifetimes searching for them. "The hidden realms remain sealed from the outer world not only by towering mountains, dense jungles, and glacier-covered passes," Sonam explained, "but by protective veils placed there by Padmasambhava [a god]. Only those with the karma to do so can enter the depths of the hidden-lands."[4]

This is the epitome of entering the World Journey to seek answers or understanding, which provides what is likely a deeper sense of enlightenment

---

3. Gray, "The Descent of Odin."
4. Baker, *The Heart of the World*, 3.

than the other triggers we've explored. In fact, "pilgrims who travel to these wild and distant places," says the Dalai Lama in *The Heart of the World*'s introduction, "often recount extraordinary experiences similar to those encountered by spiritual practitioners on the Buddhist path to Liberation....From a Buddhist perspective, sacred environments such as Pemako are not places to escape the world, but to enter it more deeply. The qualities inherent in such places reveal the interconnectedness of all life and deepen awareness of hidden regions of the mind and spirit." Entering these hidden realms invites the seeker to explore his or her innermost desires and, as the Dalai Lama says, "to discover the inner realms within which our own deepest nature lies hidden."[5] This is the ultimate point of the five locations and the seeker's progress on the World Journey.

After being triggered by one of these reasons for change (puberty, the pursuit of heroism, or the pursuit of knowledge), the seeker will make the descent. After that, their challenges lead them—we hope—to resurrection.

We All Know Resurrection

Resurrection is such a common theme that many of us might take it for granted. Myths and fairy tales are full of people going down and coming up. We expect it. The World Journey is a special type of story about people falling and then getting up again to carry on. The 2005 Christopher Nolan film *Batman Begins*, already set in a labyrinthine metropolis called Gotham, makes this point clearly. After the lead character, Bruce Wayne, falls down a well, his father utters a line that is repeated throughout the film: "Why do we fall, Bruce? So we can learn to pick ourselves up."[6] It's precisely this metaphor of rising up that makes stories so compelling and meaningful on a personal level.

Resurrection is the central theme of personal growth, and its symbolic use was likely developed by our ancestors from several fundamental human concepts and observations. Specifically, we pull the idea of personal resurrection from three perhaps surprising scientific sources: astronomy, the change of seasons, and botany. The idea is then infused into our religions. From these

---

5. Baker, *The Heart of the World*, i–10.
6. Nolan, *Batman Begins*.

four sources, the idea of resurrection has become a familiar and core plotline of World Journey stories.

Resurrection Through Astronomy

If you've ever noticed the stars' positions throughout the year, you've likely identified something that captivated our ancestors: declination. Ancient astronomers kept a close eye on the stars' position above the horizon, aware that many stars and star clusters appear on a horizon, move about the sphere of visible sky, and, at some point, sink down below the horizon only to rise into view again that night or later in the year. Circumpolar stars are those that are visible all the time when viewed from the same spot; they never dip below the horizon. For instance, the Ursa Major (Big Bear), Ursa Minor (Little Bear), and Cassiopeia constellations are always visible in most of the Northern Hemisphere.

But the further away we are from the North Pole, the more stars, clusters, and constellations dip below the horizon and demonstrate what scientists call a declination, a period during which they are out of our view due to Earth's rotation and the stars' elliptical pattern. These stars appear to dip or set (descend) in the west, disappear for hours on end, then rise in the east or dip and rise in a cyclical pattern throughout the year. This is a process that has given most non-equatorial cultures the basis for beautiful myths, such as the Egyptian myth of Nut, the sky goddess who consumes the sun in the west so that it can travel through her body and she can give birth to it in the east.

Many of these stars, including those in the constellation Orion, have a pattern of dipping and rising that corresponds to our seasons on Earth, meaning we can watch them with a certain regularity. For ancient peoples, seasons and star activity were connected in a very real and sacred way, and their patterns formed the basis of mythic stories (such as that of the regeneration goddess Venus) as well as the scientific study of astronomy.

In the same way, lunar activity has helped shape our ideas of change, constancy, and even immortality. Because the moon waxes and wanes, it is a natural symbol of resurrection. The moon dies and is reborn monthly, and early peoples (rightly) associated it with other phenomena, such as the woman who bleeds every month and yet doesn't die and the tides that surge and retreat repeatedly. Romantically, the moon is associated with the snake, which sheds its papery skin to reveal a new body underneath. Renewing itself continuously, the Serpent is thus lunar and, as we'll see, has a fascinating role in World Journey imagery.

Resurrection Through the Seasons

Just as people witnessed the story of going down and coming up by observing stars, they also saw it in the cycle of seasons. In climates that experience three or four distinct seasons, cultures have long created stories about flourishing, dying, and returning. It seems to have begun with the earliest known Mesopotamian myths of Inanna and Ishtar, glorious goddesses who descend into the depths of Hell, suffer unimaginable pain and torture, and eventually return to the Upperworld, thus creating the seasons. The later Greek story of Demeter and Persephone is a multilayered coming-of-age story that depicts both maturity and seasonal change; young Persephone descends into the Underworld, stays a few months (corresponding to the length of winter), then rises/resurrects so that her mother, the grain goddess, will preside over a new season of growing plants. Grain goddesses, such as Ceres, and the god of wine and harvest, Dionysus, were worshipped for providing the cycles of winter and summer and for offering an abundance of food and drink before the season changed and the food and drink were gone.

Resurrection Through Botany

Every biology class teaches it: The story of the seed. The plant flourishes and fruits, then the mature plant produces a seed, which falls (descends) to the ground (or travels by wind, water, bird, or fur). The seed is covered with earth, and it lies underground, silent and dark, for weeks or even months. Finally, it germinates and sends up a sprout, creating a fresh new plant. It neatly comprises the World Journey: the trigger, leaving home, descent into an unfamiliar and treacherous place (the dark Abyss), overcoming the odds, and ascending to the world even stronger than before. From this simple observation of botany, people have crafted a lasting image of renewal and regeneration.

Were it not for the seed, humanity would be bereft of imagery and also of art and literature. Cultures throughout the world sprang into being thanks to their ability to tame the wild seed and develop agriculture, feeding bellies as well as souls. The myths associated with growing plants are intricately entwined with this process of going down, staying in the dark, and rising up. Hundreds of myths of death and resurrection have been recorded from the planting cultures of Polynesia, South America, North America, Africa, Europe, Mesopotamia, and Asia. These colorful stories involve men, women, tribes, seeds, fire, babies, animals, and other relevant symbols of new life. Often, they describe threshing grains and cutting plants into pieces to be sown in the earth, such as the Egyptian story of Osiris, whose just-murdered body is viciously chopped into pieces and scattered across the land. These myths always promote the Descent-and-Resurrection story of the seed.

Resurrection Through Religion

Finally, we can relate to the idea of resurrection because it is infused into religious texts, and we have heard it throughout centuries. Taken straight from astronomy, changing seasons, and planting myths, the religious resurrection of a savior is an ancient idea and is the basis of both Christianity and Buddhism. Both Jesus and Buddha experience hardships, are thrust into dangerous and isolated situations, and emerge with new purpose. Many of the events in Jesus's life parallel earlier events in the lives of various Mesopotamian and Greek gods, including Mithras, Dionysus, and Adonis; Jesus even describes his life using the imagery of the vine.

———

Our ancestors readily internalized these concepts and used them in stories and songs, encouraging individuals to embark on journeys and in some cases even explaining how to get back home.

It's this pattern of Descent and Resurrection that makes the World Journey so effective. It's a one-two process with the first happening before the second. But the next concept we'll explore is so critical to the World Journey and personal transformation that it involves not a step-by-step process but rather a duality of seemingly opposite truths that must occur in every story: the ideas of Chaos and Void.

CHAPTER 2

Chaos and Void

Bored! Alice was bored. She sat and twiddled her thumbs and wanted to *do* something. "Alice was beginning to get very tired of sitting by her sister on the bank, and of having nothing to do."[7] So begins one of the most famous tales of personal transformation ever written, with every bored child understanding implicitly why Alice needed a change. Humans crave change, which by its definition upsets the status quo, introducing Chaos. Chaos is an element of extremity that multiplies itself on both emotional and physical levels, and Chaos has a twin sister: Void. Though it appears at first glance weak or useless, Void is another element of extremity and is every bit as powerful as Chaos; either of these will launch one's journey toward self-growth irrevocably.

For instance, consider the Forest: Many fairy tales begin with "once upon a time." And those words are most commonly followed up with the fact that the story's protagonist just went "into the woods." Hansel and Gretel went "into the woods," Little Red Riding Hood went "into the woods." This

---

7. Carroll, *Alice's Adventures in Wonderland; Through the Looking Glass; What Alice Found There; The Hunting of the Snark*, 9.

common plot point used by fairy tales describes the character walking into an element of extremity—Chaos or Void. Just as other stories use the Deep, the Cavern, the Vessel, or the Labyrinth, many fairy tales use the Forest, preparing the reader (often a child) to enter an extreme situation.

Here, we'll explore these extremes to learn how they work within the locations of the World Journey.

Chaos

Chaos implies loud noises, craziness, and feeling bewildered. Chaotic spaces are those without borders, without rules, and often full of discord and turmoil—lots of movement with no direction. In a chaotic space, one may face whirlwinds, tornadoes, hurricanes, and storms. In Chaos, there are no patterns and things feel disorganized. We feel lost, unguided, pathless. There are no rituals or ceremonies; life seems minute to minute, busy, and without plan or arrangement.

One would think Chaos and Void are exclusive and opposite. Isn't Chaos wild and loud, while Void is empty and silent? Surely one image can't be both Chaos and Void? In fact, these mythic concepts are one and the same, a duality worth exploring. Chaos is a blustery craziness in which no boundaries can be seen and no path can be discerned because there is so much *stuff*—it is a confusing and wild madness. Void is an empty desolation without form in which no boundaries can be seen and no path can be discerned because there is so much *nothingness*—it is also a confusing and wild madness. There are superficial differences: Chaos holds everything, while the Void holds nothing; Chaos contains all color, while the Void is colorless. But they are similar, too. Each is without form and shape, without border and arrangement, without pattern, and, especially, without law. Chaos and Void identify very closely in our imaginations as the liminal edge of consciousness where change happens. Each bubbles with chances, options, choices, and opportunities. Where we have Chaos or Void, we have *potential*; that is their true purpose.

Chaos is surprisingly helpful in the very creation of form and order, and it has been used as the basis of creation myths for millennia. There is so much Chaos in the Abyss that everything is a blur. In other words, it is formless. This formlessness makes it a tool not only in creation myths that revel in the image of form from formlessness but also in the experience of self-discovery; an individual seeking change is required to create pathways and order.

In literature, Chaos is a pivotal place of potential. Sometimes individuals willingly enter one of the five locations (the Cavern, the Deep, the Vessel, the Forest, or the Labyrinth) to face difficulties to prove their worth. Others are pushed in unwillingly and find themselves in a chaotic whirl of water or in a maze of trees, buildings, or people. Without warning, they are desperate to find answers amid Chaos just to survive.

Where the Void is calm and quiet, Chaos is messy. Chaotic places are confusing spaces where one is easily lost; they are dark and riddled with crossroads, intersections, paths, and stumbling blocks. Gretel in "Hansel and Gretel," the young girl in the folktale "Vasalisa," and Theseus in the Greek myth of the Minotaur move from a life of complacency, boredom, uncertainty, or innocence to enter a wild place that challenges them to the core. They must survive frightening ordeals for which there is no guidebook, or they will not progress to the next stage of life.

Our very first depiction of Chaos in literature is as the ocean, which is named "Chaos" in the ancient Babylonian poem *Enuma Elish*. This incredibly old creation story refers to the sea goddess Tiamat as Chaos herself, the Great Deep, and it pits the god of air, Marduk, against her in the first-ever epic sea battle. As the ocean, Tiamat is feminine, watery, vague, formless, deep, and emotional. She does not plan or make decisions until the fateful moment when she is threatened by the usurper Marduk, and then she brings deadly serpents from her body to attack him. But she loses the battle. Marduk murders Tiamat and forms new earth from her carcass. Tiamat is Chaos, full of potential and lacking form, but from her chaos comes firm ground. Much later, the imagery repeats in the Christian Bible story of Genesis, when "in the beginning" there is watery Chaos called "the deep," and from it, God uses his breath (air) to create order and form.[8] (Often this process is presented as gender specific: Chaos is female, while Order is male. Though this has been misconstrued to argue that women are emotional and men are rational, it really suggests that women and men can together wield the forces of potential to shape new life.)

---

8. *The Bible*, Genesis 1.

At about the same time but on the other side of the world, a creation story in Japan described the births of the goddess Izanami and the god Izanagi, who were born from "the ocean of chaos" and became the ancestral gods of all life. When they emerged from the teeming, swirling waters of the Great Deep, they stood on "the floating bridge of heaven and stirred the ocean with a jeweled spear until it curdled, and so created the first island."[9] This is a mythic way of saying the vague and watery place of potential gave way to form and shape; from Chaos the deities created Order.

In modern fiction, one of the best examples of the Abyss as Chaos is in the book *Jurassic Park*, written by Michael Creighton, and the film based on it, directed by Steven Spielberg. In this adventure, a whole bevy of characters are brought into the Abyss to learn and grow (or die trying). Jurassic Park is the ultimate Chaos; it is isolated, formless, lawless, frightening, thick with a jumble of trees and branches and vines, loud with animal sounds, and virtually pathless. The sky, land, and water are swarming with creatures of every size and description. When the protagonists' helicopter descends through the mountains and touches down in the thick of the jungle, the characters realize they have left behind their normal world of reality and have entered a terrifying place without rules or precedence. Anything could happen next, and there is no linear or established path that will help them (or us) predict what direction anyone will take. What began as an organized science project has gone wildly out of control. And in case the reference to Chaos should go undetected, one of the characters on the trip is a specialist in chaos theory: Dr. Ian Malcom, played by Jeff Goldblum in the film. This chaos theorist is constantly telling anyone who will listen that you never know what's going to happen next—in other words, that they are in a place of limitless potential. These people have left behind a structured world of conformity, complacency, or poor relationships and have entered a liminal realm filled with danger. To be specific, it's filled with dinosaurs, which are really the Serpent, an ultimate and historic image of transformation. Each person has the opportunity to make decisions that will improve (or end) his or her life, and those who succeed ascend from the deep, dark depths of the Abyss, literally

---

9. Philip, *The Illustrated Book of Myths*, 26.

lifting up in helicopters, to return to life with greater understanding, expertise, and more mature relationships.

It takes a tremendous amount of work and effort to move from Chaos into the world of form and shape to achieve self-discovery, which brings us to Chaos's counterpart, its mirror image: the Void.

The Void

A seemingly empty space, the Void is like a clear window in a wall—valuable for what is *not* present as opposed to what is. The Void is free from clutter, stuff, and obstacles of any kind. Empty, it can even be perceived as a fortifying place where we can nourish ourselves and renew fading strength, though it still holds challenges and work for the individual. Sometimes the emptiness is the very challenge one needs to face—but make no mistake, though the Void is empty, it is as much a challenge as Chaos.

An example of the Void can be found in the European fairy tale "Beauty and the Beast." When the young woman goes to live in the Beast's quiet castle, time seems to stand still for her while she manages domestic tasks. This Void is homelike and nurturing; it is a sleeplike place where Beauty, like Briar Rose and Snow White, can grow stronger before emerging into the maturity of an adult.

Even the Anglo-Saxon story of Beowulf contains elements of the Void; the story tells of Beowulf killing the dragon Grendel and then pursuing Grendel's mother down into the deep water of a lake to her lair. The lake is the Deep in this story, and it can be perceived both as the Void (it is dark, silent, and deep) and as Chaos (the water is churning with the thrashing of the dragon). But one thing is certain: the Deep is limitless potential. What will Beowulf do? The waters are full of options; the possibilities are endless. He could give up, he could find others and seek help, or he could persevere. To move into the next stage of his life, he must face the challenge of the dragon and win. As it happens, he wrestles and fights with the dragon and then spies a sword lying on the bottom of the lake. He grabs the sword, stabs the dragon, and rises up through the vague, watery depths to a new life as a hero (recall Tiamat and Marduk). He entered the Abyss, faced the challenges, and emerged stronger than ever.

One of the more intentional uses of the Void is in the final scenes of *Harry Potter and the Deathly Hallows*, after Harry presents himself to Voldemort for sacrifice. Voldemort casts his curse to kill Harry, sending him to his death. But his journey toward death, it turns out, really takes him to the Abyss, and in this case, he ends up in a liminal space that is void of sound and nearly bereft of shape or detail. It is London's King's Cross Station, though barely recognizable. It is a clean, colorless, and completely empty train station with high vaulted ceilings where, as Dumbledore tells Harry, he could easily choose his future by boarding a train and going forward. "Where would it take me?" Harry asks him. Dumbledore replies, "On."[10] This is the Void: a shapeless, vague, and formless place of potential, ripe with possibility, and serene and empty and almost sleepy enough to be a temporary place of respite. It is filled with choices, allowing the individual to attain a certain awareness or understanding before making a decision. In this place of emptiness, the individual (in this case, Harry) can assess his or her inner Self without the restrictions of judgment and social rules and has time to reflect and grow before being reborn as a conscious, helpful, useful, strong, and mature adult. This metaphor reaches us in the same way the metaphor of the Cavern does in the ancient Sumerian myth of Inanna—or any of the other stories we'll explore in this book. In the Abyss lies our potential, if only we will give shape and form to our life's purpose.

It may come as no surprise that the Void is often a prime opportunity for sleep. Author Joan Gould points out that when Sleeping Beauty becomes a budding teenager and is physically ready to begin experiencing sexuality, she is not yet mentally prepared to be a sexual adult. What does she do? She simply falls asleep. In the fairy tale, this is shown as a curse, but figuratively she is entering a void of consciousness that will allow her mind to catch up with her body so she can experience one of the most challenging transitions of her life: puberty.[11] Similarly, Snow White escapes the queen and runs "into the woods" where she undergoes an initiation involving domestic work for seven men, an initiatory experience typical of fairy tales where a young girl has nothing to look forward to as an adult but wifery and domestic servitude.

10. Rowling, *Harry Potter and the Deathly Hallows*, 722.
11. Gould, *Spinning Straw into Gold*, 87–92.

But Snow White is a young and innocent teenager; she is not ready to accept what is expected of her as an adult (or as a wife), and so what does she do? She faints into a deep sleep. Again, this is presented as a curse after eating an apple (a bloodred fruit symbolizing awareness and sexual maturity, like the pomegranate Persephone eats and the apple Eve consumes), and it is her way of withdrawing from the world for a period of time and moving inward so she can mentally and emotionally prepare herself. We *need* sleep; we need the Void, where we can return every night to quietly renew our energy and restore our strength. Dreams happen in the Void, and from these dreams we learn to aspire toward our potential.

Both Chaos and Void offer challenges and respite; each is a place of wide-open, limitless potential with no form and no direction, where the seeker can make real decisions, choose a path, and move forward.

Chaos and Void as the Same Image

Seemingly opposite, Chaos and Void are often the same thing, and our minds know it. Consider water. This element is often used as an image of the Abyss, and it handily appears as both Chaos and Void. Its dual ability to be both wild and passive, chaotic and calm, makes water a magnificent image for personal growth. Water is the Void when it is calm and reflective, a surface upon which to meditate and gain understanding, to find quiet, solitude, and the peaceful ripples of steady growth. The stories where the Abyss appears as the Vessel or as the Cauldron (see chapter 6) all show the placid mirror-surface of water as the Void. But water is also Chaos, especially in the many flood stories of ancient cultures where the devastating effects of stormy water both destroyed civilizations and welcomed new life. Each way, water as Chaos or Void consumes, reconstructs, and transforms. We'll see it as a primary image in many of the following stories of the World Journey.

Chaos and Void often appear in the same story. A film that does a great job incorporating both Chaos and Void is the popular 2014 film *The Maze Runner*, directed by Wes Ball. In the film, dozens of men and one woman are thrust into a gigantic valley where they are beset by dangers. The Valley is empty with no roads, paths, structures, or organization; it is a wide-open grassy expanse of nothingness, and the men and woman aimlessly wander across the empty valley with few objectives and no responsibilities (other than basic survival). They don't know where they are, why they are there, or how to get out. They have no memories, and their entire existence is a big question mark. They have no direction and no purpose whatsoever. This is the Void.

But when the action picks up—that is, when the lead character decides to push the known world and make more of his life—they push out through the only door and enter the Maze, which is a frightening labyrinth, just the opposite of the Valley. It has high walls, a structure of meandering and confusing corridors, left and right turns, posts and pillars and doors, choices to be made, and a jumble of directions. It is Chaos. Our job when watching the film is to recognize that both the Valley and the Maze are in fact the same image; each is the Abyss, representing a place of potential and incredible opportunity. In the film, the heroes face their monsters, make their choices, and create their escape, emerging (ironically) into a brightly lit modern room equipped with digital devices, computers, and phones. In other words, they've left the vague and formless Deep of the Self and have emerged into real, structured, *connected* life.

When we see the images of Chaos and Void appear in a story, we know the Abyss is at work and change is happening.

Entering and Leaving Chaos or Void

It's not enough to simply *be* in one of the five locations of the World Journey. The trigger that pushes a person into a new state of being is often a monumental shift in perception or experience, and the very *act* of entering or leaving the Abyss is important. When people reach a pivotal point in their lives and are ready for deep change, they must *leave* one place and *enter* the other.

Stories tell us that a person who is living in a highly emotional state of anxiety or a flurry of work must turn inward to a peaceful void; only in this way can he or she complete the necessary emotional, mental, and spiritual work needed to transform chaos to order. Similarly, a person experiencing nothing of value and feeling empty, bored, or lost must enter a place (either literal or figurative) of stimulation to excite change. We all experience such transitions in life. For instance, a busy workaholic may literally travel somewhere, such as a silent meditation retreat center, to experience a shift in consciousness. But she will also need to go inward metaphorically to allow her conscious self to access that liminal space of unconsciousness so her inner mind can move past stasis and achieve change. To do this, we leave one state of being and enter either Chaos or Void.

The world's stories are brimming with these pivotal departures; it is at this titillating point that the excitement begins, and we see the seeker start to change his or her experience. King Arthur and his knights depart on their grand quest, leaving a place of relative security to enter the vast lands of the unknown, trekking across misty heaths and tangled meadows to seek the Grail of Enlightenment (a Vessel, see chapter 6). At a pivotal point in their lives, both Jesus and Buddha leave the comfort of their homes to enter the desolate Void of a desert and the Chaos of a forest, respectively, where they face challenges that test them.

We see two departures from the ordinary in Victor Fleming's 1939 film *The Wizard of Oz,* based on L. Frank Baum's book. The first is a frightening experience when Dorothy leaves her boring Kansas home in the terror of a tornado, landing in a confusing and maddening world completely foreign to her. She shifts from Void to Chaos. The second is a moment of celebration when she is placed on the first steps of the Yellow Brick Road and is sent off on her journey, leaving the cacophony of meaningless songs and empty smiles to dance blithely into the dark, quiet unknown on a path that stretches out into the nothingness. Each time, she is entering the Abyss— the first through Chaos, the second through Void. Similarly, consider both the rabbit hole in *Alice's Adventures in Wonderland* and the bizarre alien bar in George Lucas's 1977 film *Star Wars*. Each is the entry point to the limitless, liminal Abyss, the launching pad from which the hero leaves the ordinary and enters the extraordinary, the edge over which whatever falls is bound to change.

Emerging from the Abyss is often just as frightening a process as entering. Emerging, or resurrecting, is what finally brings form to the formless, and in stories, curiously, this is often signaled with the giving of names. As the *Enuma Elish* says of the Void at the beginning of creation, "When on high the heaven had not been named, Firm ground below had not been called by name...none bore a name, and no destinies (determined)."[12] Only after changing from chaos to firmament is the goddess Tiamat named.

---

12. Davis, *Don't Know Much about Mythology,* 136.

Names and fulfillment happen *after* one has resurrected. We see this in the Greek myth of Persephone. Kore descends into the Abyss as an innocent girl, but when she emerges, she is named Persephone. In the Torah, Abram's name is changed to Abraham and Sarai's name is changed to Sarah, indicating their new stature and sacred responsibility. Upon attaining enlightenment, Siddhartha Gautama becomes the Buddha. Naming a person with either a new name or a new title indicates that this person has transitioned from one thing into something else entirely. They have left behind something old and have taken up a new identity or, at a minimum, a new perception of identity that leads to strength, maturity, and fulfillment.

The tremendous transformation that moves a person from one level of being to another requires time spent in the formlessness of Chaos and Void, the two equal-but-opposite aspects of the Journey. Their lack of form and structure indicates they are potential—*opportunity*—and ripe with possibility. Next, we'll identify another set of dual concepts without which no traveler on the World Journey would ever survive: the Beast and the Guide.

CHAPTER 3

The Beast and the Guide

There is one more extreme encountered on the World Journey that is utterly frightening and yet crucially necessary. This is experienced as another duality, a pair of opposites, and is perhaps the most important of all. These are twin beings—personas, if you will—who prove to be the two most influential beings we may ever encounter. Just like Descent and Resurrection and Chaos and Void, which are opposites yet equal, these personas oppose each other yet are identical in many ways; we will call them the Beast and the Guide.

Along the World Journey, these may appear as people, as living animals, or as magical creatures. Regardless of the form they take, the Beast and the Guide are so important they will influence us more than anything else on our journey—and almost without exception, in myths, fairy tales, and modern fiction and film, we encounter not just one but *both*. The Beast is often the most difficult challenge—it wants to eat you, to utterly devour you, because you cannot change unless you are symbolically eaten and transformed. The Guide is your support person and will help you navigate your way out of the Abyss—which is the essence of resurrection.

You may think, "I've never been attacked by a symbolic beast who wants to eat me!" Or more tragically, you may think, "I've never had a guide." But according to stories, we experience both—and we need both to travel upon the road of change. Let's examine them here.

The Wolf, the Witch, and the Whale: The Beasts That Consume

In the netherworlds around Oz, Dorothy encountered wicked beasts such as flying monkeys, lions, and strange animals in their fiercest forms. In our own lives, we face the wretched, confusing, and challenging situations that are analogous to the beasts in these tales. These circumstances leave us stronger than before, as facing these situations helps us become more mature and able to look at the world with a new purpose or a fresh perspective. But we generally can't do it alone. Humans need symbols—images that trick the brain and engage the imagination—to cloak our pain in a way that helps us manage our minds and hearts. The entire point of many stories and myths written or carved into stone millennia ago was to clothe these familiar but painful life challenges in the sheepskin of symbol and teach us how to survive.

We meet the Beast when we're at the core of the World Journey—unquestionably the most dreadful and scariest times of one's life. In the tales we explore in this book, the Beast may be a witch, a serpent, a whale, a wolf, a dragon, or a god or goddess. It can also be other people and the folly of human nature. Regardless of the form it takes, the Beast is there for one reason and one reason only. To be sure, the Beast is frightening, but it serves a much deeper function than simply scaring us. The Beast is not there to teach us a lesson or prove a moral point. In fact, the Beast introduces two critical concepts that we tend to ignore because they are too painful or unnerving to even consider: the ideas of *consummation* and *sacrifice*.

What Does It Mean to Sacrifice?

The concept of sacrifice is the pivotal deed without which no person can change. Dictionaries define *sacrifice* as the offering of an animal, plant, or human life to a deity or the surrender of something prized for the sake of something having a higher value. Sacrifice refers to the giving up of something cherished in exchange for the promise of something even better, and it can be given freely, or it can be forced. Religious texts and myths are full of stories of animal and human sacrifices to please a deity—but there are just as many stories of people willingly giving up something precious to gain something better, of people leaving a cherished home for the promise of a new land, and of men and women accepting the blame for crimes of which they are innocent to protect someone they love.

These sacrifices show humanity at its most gracious and tender, but there is one image of sacrifice that gets directly to the heart of what it means to grow and mature: when men and women surrender themselves to be eaten by the Beast. To be clear, the Beast does not represent evil; the World Journey has nothing to do with giving oneself up to evil thoughts and values. Rather, surrendering to the Beast is a metaphor for developing the courage needed to recognize the best part of yourself. In this context and throughout literature, surrendering to the greatest challenge one can imagine is allowing oneself to change. And oddly, in literature, to be consumed is the truest way to experience a new chance in life and, even, to glimpse immortality. Physically entering one of the five locations of the World Journey is the first step and facing its challenges may be the second—each is a type of surrender—but meeting and surrendering to the Beast is the strongest act of personal sacrifice. Curiously and emphatically, it involves *being eaten*.

In stories, it's quite dramatic. The authors of stories throughout time have pitted heroes against terribly ugly, dismal, and cunning characters, making the seekers work especially hard to gain their reward. But no character is quite as alarming, quite as nasty—or quite as effective—as the one that literally eats the hero alive: the Beast. Nearly every story of transformation features the hero being *consumed* in the flesh, *eaten* by the thing that is most fearsome, *swallowed* down the gullet of a beast that has no remorse or feeling of guilt. In fact, the Beasts in most myths and fairy tales take great delight in eating the hero—taunting him or her before attacking and swallowing them whole.

Being Consumed on the World Journey

To be clear, a sacrifice must be tremendous to truly be effective. A sacrifice is no small pittance—no self-respecting Beast will accept a trinket or a payment of money or even a small body part. In fact, the sacrifice demanded by the Beast is surprisingly clear. One must be eaten bodily, consumed in one's entirety. This requirement is universal, and it teaches what is probably the most important lesson of the World Journey—that giving yourself completely to something will ultimately transform you. Giving of the entire Self cannot be avoided if one is to change. It is terrifying and, on its surface, appears to be a great tragedy, but afterward, what happens? In nearly every tale, the hero does not suffer failure. To the contrary, the hero not only survives but flourishes, emerging transformed.

Unfortunately, modern adaptations of these stories have glossed over the magnitude of the experience of being eaten. Today's children watch movies in which the hero or heroine is figuratively "slapped on the wrist" instead of facing true transformative beasts. But the older and original stories held nothing back, making it clear that the person in question was consumed, body and soul. Jonah is swallowed entirely by the whale. Little Red Riding Hood (and her grandmother, too) are consumed by the wolf. The dragons in the tales of Saint George and various Grimm stories eat virgin girls (whose transformation is either puberty or marriage), and the witch in the candy-covered house gleefully eats children, caging them and cooking them in her oven. Many recent adaptations shy away from this image of being eaten and merely hint that the intention of the Beast is to eat the child. The idea of a witch, a wolf, or a whale eating someone is often touted as distasteful and not for children's stories. But this is precisely the metaphor that is so important in stories that show a character's transformation.

But if the hero is eaten, isn't he dead? Actually—no. It is vitally important to recognize that the Beast does not simply want to kill the hero. Killing results in death, and it is the end. Instead of killing the hero, the Beast wants to eat him or her. Why? Because eating is a cyclic act; once eaten, the flesh feeds another, resulting in new life. Eating is an act of regeneration. Communities that eat together thrive; meals are the cornerstone of family and cultural events for a reason. Eating not only resolves hunger but is both a communal and a ceremonial act, and it is literally transformative, taking the flesh or body of one living being and using it to create and nourish someone new. When the hero of the story is eaten or faces the threat of being eaten, it is symbolic of great change—it is not death but ultimate renewal. We'll see this image of eating clearly when we explore the location of the Vessel, since eating the soup brewed in a cauldron is a popular way to initiate change.

Coming of Age: Being Eaten as an Act of Sexual Maturity

If we look closely, we can see that many of the stories of growth and personal transformation harken not to changing one's ways but simply to reaching a new stage of life. Some tales in which a Beast downs the hero through the gullet symbolize rites of sexual maturity. Two European tales depict the concept of being eaten by the Beast in a way that highlights the process of puberty.

The first is "Saint George and the Dragon," a story from early Anatolian myth and later repeated in European literature in which George battles a dragon that is terrorizing a village. The villagers feed the dragon two sheep daily, but when the sheep run out, they feed the beast their virgin daughters. When all the other girls in the kingdom have been eaten, the king's daughter is finally dressed as a new bride and is about to be fed to the dragon—but George appears and saves the day. Compare this story of a maiden being eaten by the Beast to the second European tale, "Little Red Riding Hood."

Charles Perrault, the author who first recorded the children's tale in writing, knew a thing or two about wolves, and he wasted no time clarifying to families in the late 1600s that wolves (in other words, lusty men) existed among them in their very homes. Perrault, a wealthy aristocrat in Paris, devoted his later years to preserving oral European folktales for his children, stories which had been passed down perhaps for centuries. It's thanks to him that we have *Cinderella: Or, The Little Glass Slipper*, *Blue Beard*, *Sleeping Beauty*, *Little Red Riding Hood*, and *Puss in Boots*—published in 1697 by him under the pseudonym Mother Goose. Perrault's written versions of these old tales did not shy away from the violence inherent in the warnings. In fact, he kept all the gory details, including Beauty's stepmother wanting to eat her, Snow White being hunted by the evil queen who wishes to eat her heart, and Little Red Riding Hood encountering the "sly old fellow."[13]

As Perrault wrote it, more than 100 years prior to the Brothers Grimm recording their tales, the virgin maiden leaves her home, enters the forest, and arrives at her grandmother's house. She finds the wolf disguised and lying in the bed, and when he invites her to "come into bed," the girl willingly undresses and goes to the bedside where the wolf eats her whole. "From

13. Perrault, *Tales of Passed Times*.

this story," Perrault cautioned at the end of the tale, "one learns that children, especially young lasses, pretty, courteous, and well-bred, do very wrong to listen to strangers, and it is not an unheard thing if the Wolf is thereby provided with his dinner."[14] To this day, "seeing the wolf" is a French euphemism for "losing one's virginity" or experiencing the transformation from a girl to a sexual woman.[15] The young girl, Little Red, is eaten by the Beast—consumed, in fact—and *consummation* still refers to the sexual act, especially on a bride and groom's wedding night when the maiden is transformed into a married woman.

It may seem inappropriate to include stories of sex or virginity in children's tales, but the act of sexual consummation has long held fascination for clergy members, family, and friends, and it has even influenced politics. Cultures around the world have scrutinized a couple's activities of sex and consummation, with the bride and groom being escorted to their marriage bed in celebration with others observing everything possible save the act of sexual intercourse itself and sometimes even that. Activities in elite marriage beds in England, Germany, Scandinavia, and elsewhere, especially in the Middle Ages, were far-from-private ceremonial affairs. Tales such as "Little Redcap," which was recounted by Charles Perrault and later renamed "Little Red Riding Hood" by the Brothers Grimm, grew out of an oral story custom that warned and prepared teenage girls to accept the (perhaps distasteful and painful) overtures of their new (and perhaps old, ugly, deformed, or violent) husbands on their wedding night and beyond.

The consummation is, in every sense, a total transformation. In both stories, a girl surrenders herself physically to a beast and emerges from the experience completely changed, transformed into a woman or "bride," a loose fictional veil over a very real experience for far too many girls throughout history. She is transformed emotionally, socially, and physically, having been both physically penetrated and ritually consumed. Is it a change for the better? This question was rarely asked. It was simply the way it was done. And though Christians edited George's ancient tale so that "Saint" George compels all the villagers to convert to Christianity before he agrees to kill the

---

14. Perrault, "Little Red Riding Hood."
15. Lawson, "Cape Fear."

dragon, thus giving the tale religious connotations, it is nevertheless a story of being consumed as a coming-of-age experience. In the tale, the monster that George slaughters is a dragon (a form of the Serpent) that represents numerous things to the subconscious human mind:

- darkness and death
- feminine regenerative powers of creativity thanks to its reptilian association with serpents of immortality
- the challenges a girl must face and the sacrifices she must make when she transitions from a child into a woman (and specifically into a wife)
- the creative (regenerative) subconscious of the human spirit, which must be fed in order to grow

As we'll explore further, the Serpent is all of these things, and depending on our own personal adventure and cultural values, we perceive multiple meanings.

It is interesting to note that this story of George and the dragon has two heroes who each undergo a personal transformation: George, who battles the dragon and emerges as a hero, and the king's daughter, who prepares to be "fed to the dragon" and transitions from a maiden to a bride.

The Consuming Beast: The Wolf, the Witch, and the Serpent

Generally, stories use metaphors to refer to actual human foibles that the seeker must correct or grow from, as they are easier to understand and they make for a more memorable story. In the world of myth, tale, and film, there are three primary metaphorical Beasts that continually show up to wreak the most havoc. They are the Wolf, the Witch, and the Serpent, or the Whale.

The Wolf

Often a key character in stories of the Forest, the Wolf, or the Fox, is cunning and smart. He is wily and may perch nearby, as he does in Beatrix Potter's *The Tale of Jemima Puddle-Duck*, casually reading a newspaper as Jemima Puddle-Duck innocently moves her eggs to his nest. In this story, he wears a handsome waistcoat and is ever so charming, inviting Jemima to make her nest past the edge of the garden, far away from the farm and on the edge of the dark woods. But given the chance, he would pounce on her and eat the eggs.

In one of Aesop's fables, the Greek storyteller teaches morality through the lesson of a shepherd boy who falsely cries wolf. The boy amuses himself by lying, and the villagers grow frustrated with him. But later, when a wolf really does appear and snatches away his sheep, the boy calls for help and no villagers come. The wolf in this tale doesn't eat the boy but helps him grow up quickly by learning a lesson about truth telling. Much later, in 1936, the Russian symphony performance *Peter and the Wolf* was written by Sergei Prokofiev and later adapted by Walt Disney to an animated film. In the original symphony, Peter is a disobedient boy who defies his grandfather's warning to stay inside because of a wolf seen nearby. Peter sneaks out and manages to capture the wolf, showing stubbornness rather than growth. A later adaptation performed by the Philharmonic Orchestra has Peter freeing the wolf and walking with him side by side.

Perhaps the best-known appearance of the Wolf as the Beast is in the European fairy tale "Little Red Riding Hood." Like this well-known tale, another Grimm tale called "The Wolf and the Seven Kids" portrays the Wolf as a cunning and sly murderer who changes his appearance in order to fool the kids. When the kids' mother, a nanny goat, leaves the house, she warns them, "Beware of the wolf! If once he gets into the house, he will eat you up—skin, and hair, and all. The rascal often disguises himself, but you will know him by his rough voice and his black feet."[16] Sure enough, the wolf presents himself at the window, and the kids deny him entry because of his deep voice, but he purchases chalk and swallows it, which makes his voice softer. Again, the kids deny him entry because they see his dark paw, but the wolf persuades a baker to cover his paw in bread dough and flour, and so he fools the children. Once in, he eats them all except for the littlest.

Often straightforward and easy to identify, the Wolf is a caricature that we can all recognize when we see it in our daily lives. It is someone who is false, pretends to be something they are not, disguises their true nature, and

---

16. The Brothers Grimm, *Grimm's Fairy Tales*, 140.

does not have our best interest at heart. In stories, the Wolf is one of the three Beasts that presses a character to change. The next, equally horrifying and influential, is the Witch.

The Witch

In the story of Hansel and Gretel, the witch tells Gretel about her plans for her brother, saying, "I want to fatten him up, and when he's fat enough, I'm going to eat him."[17] In Japan, scary stories are told of the old mountain hag Yama Uba who eats lost travelers. And writer and professor Veronique Tadjo shares folktales from Africa's Ivory Coast, describing "an old witch" who eats people's souls.[18]

Hundreds of years of storytelling have typecast the old woman as a witch, and usually she is harrowing. She is often described as simultaneously very old and very young—again, the opposites of Chaos and Void, where the old face full of wrinkles and warts is indistinguishable from the fresh youthful face of the Void. But in stories throughout time and across many cultures, she does not merely injure a person or frighten a person or even kill someone. Instead, she eats him or her, devouring the victim whole. Many a text and tale introduce an appealing, persuasive, yet ultimately horrifying witch whose main intent is to eat the hero. She beguiles the hero into entering her home, hut, or cave, and once they cross the threshold, consummation begins.

Just as the wolf is the Beast who eats Little Red Riding Hood, so is the witch who attempts to eat Hansel. Hansel is only saved at the last minute by his sister's smart thinking. Similarly, in a Russian folktale, the witch Baba Yaga warns Vasalisa that if she does not finish her tasks, she will eat her up. In a Welsh myth, the deity Cerridwen disguises herself as an old woman and then changes her form multiple times. She eats the young boy Gwion after he steals drops of wisdom from her cauldron; he transforms into a grain of corn and she into a hen. She literally consumes him, giving birth to him later as Taleisin, or Merlin. (You can read more of their story in chapter 6, "The Vessel.") And in Snow White, the queen sends her huntsman to bring back the heart and liver of the girl, which the queen eats, believing

---

17. Zipes, *The Original Folk and Fairy Tales of the Brothers Grimm*, 47.
18. Blair, "Why Are Old Women Often the Face of Evil in Fairy Tales and Folklore?"

she is consuming at least part of the child. It is suggested that the queen wants to ingest some of the youthful properties of the girl, but as is shown in other tales, the metaphor of consummation tells us that being eaten is Snow White's transition, her "awakening" on the path of adulthood.

To be consumed by the Beast is to morph entirely, to pass through one phase of being into another. In fact, the Witch is dying to consume the girl— Baba Yaga is both Chaos and Void, waiting to swallow the hero into her gullet, never to be seen again—unless the hero wins, changes, and wakes up to pull from her stores of strength and passion so that true transformation can occur. When we encounter the Witch in these stories, we are looking at the transformative agent of change; she is the Beast who will acknowledge one's sacrifice by eating the old part of a person and spitting it out in a new form.

And while the Wolf, the Witch, and the Serpent each represent the vehicle of terrible, deep, and utterly transformative change in a person's journey, symbolizing the frightening monster we must face (the decision, the choice, or the action), the last one on this list—the Serpent—is a much more versatile image. The Wolf and the Witch are rather straightforward; they are an animal and a human and are generally recognizable. But the Serpent refers to multiple images that reach deep into history and affect us in profound and startling ways.

The Serpent

Ah, the Snake. It is hard to explore the imagery of personal transformation without looking at the Snake. The Serpent is as widespread in our myths and tales as any symbol could possibly be and is perhaps the most well-known and the most feared. It is powerful and integral precisely because it is so effective at teaching change and spiritual growth.

The Serpent enjoys a dynamic history as an agent of change. The Serpent is everywhere because it is so versatile, taking a surprising number of forms in myth, text, and tale. It is a snake in the stories of Adam and Eve and Jason and the Fleece. It is a dragon in countless Chinese tales and a sea monster in the Old Testament stories of Tiamat and the Leviathan. It is the basilisk in Harry Potter, an almost pet snake that can "speak" to our inner desires, and it is a reptilian sea monster, sea beast, or "giant fish" that swallows a man whole in the story of Jonah.

The Serpent even appears as a crocodile (think of *Peter Pan*), and in fairy tales it is toned down a bit and portrayed as a toad ("The Princess and the Frog" or the animal tales penned by Madame d'Aulnoy), but it is always the slithering or swimming reptilian beast that must be faced before the conscious human spirit can grow. In each of its many forms and in cultures around the world, the Serpent has very specific duties:

– It is an aspect of feminine creation and re-birthing thanks to the sea serpent's association with water and sea deities.

– It represents immortality because snakes shed their skin repeatedly, being "reborn," and it is the guardian of the Sacred Tree of Life.

– It compels the creative urge of human thought and poetic impulse, being that which must awaken from within.

– Finally, the Serpent is the Beast, representing the consuming challenges that heroes must face and the sacrifices that must be made when they plumb the depths of the unconscious to realize a stronger and more compassionate identity.

Let's strip the Snake of its skin and explore each of these more fully.

The Dragon as the Deep: The Female Birther

Hollywood has toyed with the imagery of the Dragon as a male beast, a destructive force of testosterone that can eliminate entire villages. But throughout mythic literature, the Dragon (representing the Serpent) is feminine. It is a vestige of the Deep, that salty oceanic womb of life and rebirth, and as such, it is uniquely feminine. Sometimes film directors like to trick the audience by revealing that the fearsome dragon is really female by showing her protecting an egg. In fact, in most literature throughout time, the Dragon or Serpent represents the feminine qualities of rebirth, or it is closely associated with a young woman growing physically or spiritually.

It is out of the feminine depths of the ancient Abyss that the Dragon or Serpent emerges—doing so quite literally in the *Enuma Elish*, a strange and wonderful story from Mesopotamia (see chapter 5). In the *Enuma Elish*, the sea serpent emerges from the body of the goddess of the ocean, Tiamat;

from this tale forward, many cultures have identified the ocean as female. (Later, goddess imagery was subdued and sky or sun gods got the credit for birthing new beings, a clear shift away from the feminine.) The Serpent's connection with water is central to its message of renewal and rebirth. Many dragon stories combine water and serpents; the seeker leaves dry land (or his village), comes to the edge of a lake or the sea, and encounters a serpent or sea monster of the Deep. Here, he requires the assistance (and consummation) of the goddess to move forward in his life.

Because the ocean is home to enormous and mysterious creatures that exist in real life—giant and colossal squid and sperm whales, among others—people tend to imagine other fantastic creatures in the dark, watery depths, too. People have imagined mermaids; the octopus-like Hydra; the Scottish Loch Ness Monster; the Norse sea serpent Jörmungandr; the Greek Gorgon Medusa, a daughter of a marine deity; the Kraken of Scandinavian folklore; and many more. Literature is awash with stories of sailors battling terrifying and monstrous sea dragons and serpents and either surviving or perishing; these stories go back to the most ancient times, with the Hebrew story of the mighty serpent Leviathan being one of the most influential. The Book of Job says of the Leviathan that "he is king over all proud beasts." The serpent "with fearsome teeth" and "who makes the depths boil like a pot" with smoke from his nostrils clearly evokes the image of a dragon. Part snake, part flying beast, he snorts and has horrible breath that "sets coals ablaze" and flames that dart from his mouth.[19] In the Book of Isaiah, he is called the wriggling serpent, and every implication is that this formidable beast can only be killed by God or his heroes.

Aboriginal peoples of Australia also connect the snake with the element of water. They do so in a more positive if also more sexual way, telling of the life-giving Rainbow Snake or Serpent that travels across the land in the lovely form of a rainbow bestowing water. Interestingly, these myths have an element of the Beast in them, as the serpent is said to devour a group of sisters who are swimming in a pool. The serpent regurgitates the sisters back up out of its body, a feminine birthing act that creates firm land.[20] In

19. *Saint Joseph Edition of the New American Bible*, 627.
20. Ions, *The History of Mythology*, 139.

some Aboriginal stories, the serpent idles in pools of water, depositing "spirit children" like semen, which impregnate the women who swim there.[21] In all these tales, the Serpent is the agent of change and rebirth.

But isn't the Serpent fearsome? How can a terrible beast symbolize rebirth and creativity? Though it seems counter to modern ideas of happy birth and innovation, in many cultures, the Serpent is celebrated as a positive feminine force capable of generating new life, likely because a snake sheds its skin throughout its life to renew itself. And though ancient readers of the *Enuma Elish* and the Bible viewed the defeat of the Serpent as a masculine victory over feminine chaos, not every interpretation of the Serpent implies that chaos must be defeated.

One Norse story celebrates the Dragon not as chaos but as personal creativity and includes the idea of "being eaten by the Beast" but with a twist. Instead of the Serpent eating the hero, the Norse story of Sigurd (also called Siegfried) presents it the other way around; when Sigurd killed a dragon in battle, he roasted its heart, but he burned his finger and, like in the Welsh tale of Fionn, he stuck his burned and bloody finger in his mouth. Instantly, he "gained the power to understand birds" and renewed his life.[22] In consuming the blood of the dragon, he pulled into his own identity that which the dragon represents: rebirth and higher consciousness. One is not consumed but is consuming; it is not a slaying but a metamorphosis.

The Serpent as the Vehicle of Immortality

Thanks to its watery and feminine image as a regenerator, the Serpent is also imagined as a vehicle of immortal life—not simply *new* life but *never-ending* life, similar to that experienced by the gods. Since the Serpent appears as the familiar snake, capable of shedding its skin and thus birthing itself anew, it is sometimes depicted with its tail gripped in its mouth, forming a never-ending circle, a symbol of eternity. These metaphors imply that death is not final and that life will continue, whether in this world or in another dimension that may very well be accessible via the World Journey.

---

21. Strang, "Life Down Under."
22. Ions, *The History of Mythology*, 65.

In another cosmic image of immortality, the Snake is seen winding up a tree, perhaps coiled around the Tree of Life, upward and upward in a never-ending spiral. Like water, the Tree is an image of immortality and expanded consciousness (more on the Tree in chapter 7), and together the Serpent and the Tree are an undeniable arrow pointing to everlasting life—not never dying but eternal truth. Identified as the Tree Guardian, the magical Serpent is a magnificently powerful image in both religious and medical connotations.

The Serpent as Tree Guardian

It is one of the most ancient and recognizable pairings in the human collection of symbols: the Snake and the Tree. Coiled among its branches, hanging from its limbs, spiraling up its trunk, and proffering its fruit, the Serpent appears as guardian and extension of the Tree of Life. As Tree Guardian, the Serpent binds itself to an established image of connection to the upper- and underworlds, linking mortality and immortality, hopelessness and rebirth.

The symbol of the Sacred Tree is an ancient and pan-cultural image that relates many hard-to-grasp ideas: universal inclusion, collective understanding, inner consciousness, and mystical dimensions of thought and human experience. All this from one tree? In fact, the image is so universal we have come to accept it as a natural "given" that the Tree (and a Forest of trees) encompasses so many lofty meanings. By itself, the Tree symbolizes eternal life and in some biblical texts is explicitly named the Tree of Life, just to be sure we understand. But when it is paired with another symbol of regeneration such as a snake? Now the image is doubly strong; the Tree keeping company with the Serpent is the ultimate image of surrender, sacrifice, and renewal.

To include one or the other of these images in a story would be profound, but including both knocks the story's meaning off the charts. The Tree of Life and the Serpent of Immortality together form an important allusion that can't be missed when reading myths, texts, and folktales. Together, they refer to the sacrifice and ultimate resurrection of the spirit, something myths have long sought to explain. They also refer to self-discovery and transition from one state of being to the next, something fairy tales are very good at.

We see these dual pairings in many places.

In the Hebrew Bible

Genesis shows the Serpent acting as the Beast. Renaissance artist Albrecht Dürer painted the snake as dangling enticingly from the branches of the Tree of the Knowledge of Good and Evil, urging Eve to rebel by eating the tree's fruit. To eat the fruit would open Eve's eyes to the knowledge of good and evil, likely an experiential understanding of real life. It would also cast her out of the Garden of Eden. Eve's rebellious act—listening to the serpent—sacrifices her safety and the familiar stasis of the Garden of Eden. As Beast, the Serpent is responsible for eating the hero or being eaten by the hero. Though the serpent does not eat Eve, it gives her the fruit of change, an image reflected in the even older Sumerian story of Inanna drinking the waters of life in the Underworld and later by Persephone eating the pomegranate fruit in the Underworld. The water and the fruit are the vehicles of change, and in Eve's story, change is provided by the serpent.

But the serpent is not in the garden alone; it is there specifically wrapped around the Sacred Tree, a combination that makes its role much more profound than simply coaxing a rebellion. The serpent is not just inciting disorder—it is guiding Eve toward enlightenment by placing in her hands the tool she needs to grow. In this way, the serpent is not only the Beast but also the Guide, an intriguing happenstance in many fairy tales where the instigator of change also shows the path to order. To grow and mature, Eve must accept the challenge offered by the serpent by sacrificing part of herself—the innocent, childish, and helpless part. She is kicked out of Eden and becomes mortal, but ironically this allows her to become a baby-producing progenitor of future generations. In other words, as a mother of infinite generations, she symbolically becomes immortal. As the agent of change and growth, the serpent shares with Eve the information she needs to make important decisions about growth, change, and maturity. Through these acts, Eve gains enlightenment.

In Greek Myths

The Greeks loved the image of the Serpent and infused their stories with all sorts of serpents, including snakes, serpent-like dragons, pythons, and other creatures—many of which were tree guardians and, as such, were guardians to portals of the Underworld. Countless Greek myths portray the Serpent as the sacred guardian of the gate of change, often connected with apple trees. The following examples share the fascination people have long had regarding serpents that guard trees, especially fruit trees. This mythic image shows up in a variety of ways that pair snakes and specifically apple trees, an association that extends much further in the past than Adam and Eve.

- Hydra: This serpent-dragon or water beast lived in Lake Lerna, serving as a many-headed guardian of a portal to the Underworld in both Greek and Roman myths.
- Python: The earth-dragon Python is a chthonic (underworld) monster. When Apollo slays it, its corpse falls into a chasm. The famous historic oracle priestess Pythia is said to have built her station above the chasm and over Python's corpse to prophesy the future. Other oracles followed suit, using snakes as a divination tool, a process that continues today in a distantly related form of snake handling in some branches of the Pentecostal church.
- Ladon: This terrible and many-headed dragon guards the Tree of Golden Apples at the entrance to the Underworld at the Garden of the Hesperides.
- A fearsome dragon guards the golden fleece that hangs on an apple tree at Colchis—the same fleece sought by Jason of the Argonauts. It is said to be the same dragon famously enchanted by Medea/Athena/Hecate for Jason.

The Religious and Mythic Pairing of Serpents and Trees

Why do so many cultures revere trees and especially fruit trees? And why does it take a serpent, of all creatures, to protect them? Because the Sacred Tree itself has branches that touch Heaven (a place of mystery) and at the same time roots that penetrate deep in the Underworld (a portal of death and rebirth). The Tree represents the physical and spiritual connection to other dimensions and—in many ancient cultures—it represents feminine consciousness. While the Serpent represents either male enlightenment or feminine regeneration—and the cyclic promise of immortality—the Tree symbolizes the fruitful life-giving goddess with its red or golden apple of wisdom.

Ancient Egyptians and Assyrians carved countless reliefs of the Sacred Tree on the walls of tombs and imprinted trees on the cylinder seals of clay jars. The gods Isis and Osiris were believed to have emerged from the trunk of an acacia tree, or Tree of Life. The Asherah of the Old Testament refers to the Tree of Life of the goddess Asherah, Ashtoreth, or Ishtar, often found growing or planted on the mountaintops, though the Tree image was whittled down into a mere stake or pole by the time goddess worship was condemned by the Hebrews. Only in Genesis is the Tree's imagery of immortality twisted to portray *morality*. There, the Tree is used to teach moral right or wrong instead of growth and enlightenment, the Serpent is the deceitful betrayer of humankind instead of the necessary agent of change, and Eve is the immoral and weak sinner instead of the progenitor of humankind and the image of ultimate motherhood. Despite the centuries of blame and guilt heaped upon this ancient story, we can still glean that Eve's act of taking the fruit tree's apple from the serpent and eating it is the result of the Beast and the Guide.

In Medicine
Imagery of the Serpent even shows up in our views of healing. This is not surprising given that in healing the sick body, we are trying to restore life and delay death, and the snake shedding its skin is the perfect metaphor. One of the chief symbols of medicine and healing is the Greek staff of Asclepius in which a snake coils up a stake or pole, paralleling the Tree of Life. In ancient Greece, the snake was not only symbolic but highly practical; its flesh and venom were pounded, extracted, and dried for use in medications and antidotes.

The Serpent as the Beast
Because it symbolizes rebirth and immortality, one of the primary functions of the Serpent is to be the Beast. The Serpent as Beast is dire, dark, and challenging. It is fearsome and frightening. It swallows people whole and—this is the important part—it spits them back out. Whether we want to or not, the Serpent forces us to do the seemingly impossible work that must be done in the liminal space of the Deep to achieve personal growth. In some stories, this work is violent and takes physical strength, such as killing or

defeating the Serpent, and it is frightening and life-threatening, resulting in the sacrifice of arms or legs. This is unlike fairy tales, where the work is less physical and more about moral fortitude—cleaning house and shaking the feather bed with honesty and integrity.

A battle against a serpent has been the pivotal coming-of-age story for boys the way most fairy tales are coming-of-age stories for young women. The tales of Beowulf and Marduk, for example, are designed to support the rite of passage for boys, and they use the allure of the Serpent as Beast to achieve their desired effect. Whether it is for puberty or maturity, the Serpent can be both the Beast and the Guide.

Jonah and the Whale

There's one story that takes the image of the sea monster to the extreme: Jonah and the Whale. Not only do we find a hero who descends, but just in case we missed the message about personal transformation, he is outright eaten by the Beast, making it one of the most enduring stories about complete surrender, redemption, and rebirth.

In this ancient tale, Jonah is called out by God to travel to Nineveh with the purpose of convincing its citizens to repent for their sins. But instead of going immediately to Nineveh to fulfill the command, Jonah chickens out, detours to a nearby port, boards a ship, and joins the crew in sailing to faraway Tarshish. Does Jonah start to feel guilty? Apparently, because the crew notices his guilty demeanor and grows suspicious when their ship is overtaken by a violent storm. The sailors draw lots to determine which of them caused the storm, and it is found to be Jonah, of course, who has displeased God. He doesn't deny it.

In fact, he demands the sailors throw him overboard to save themselves. At first, they are reluctant, yet as the storm ravages their ship, they find it reasonable, and they heave cowardly Jonah overboard. Quickly, on the surface of the water, the storm calms. But below, Jonah sinks down into the dark depths and soon—unnervingly—he finds himself passing over the lips and teeth of a giant fish. A whale has opened its great maw and swallowed him whole. Trapped in the pitch-black darkness of the belly of the great fish of the Deep, Jonah floats aimlessly. He prays to God to release him, making all sorts of promises—perhaps truly repenting and vowing to change his ways—and after three wet, waterlogged, miserable days, God commands the great fish to vomit him up onto shore. Jonah has barely shaken himself dry when God's voice again commands him to travel to Nineveh to convince its citizens to repent.

"Buried" for three days and three nights and miraculously brought back to life and light? The story of Jonah and the Whale must be important, as it is included in the texts of three major religions: in the Septuagint (the Greek translation of the Jewish Old Testament), the Christian Bible, and the Islamic Qur'an. Even Matthew in the New Testament compares the experience of Jonah to the resurrection of Jesus, so it is no surprise that this tale is one of the best-known stories of Descent and Resurrection ever shared. Today, we typically refer to this beast as a whale, but the original Hebrew text reads *dag gadol* (big fish), and the Septuagint translates this into the Greek *ketos mega*. To the Greeks, this more accurately described a sea monster or sea serpent.

Today, writers and filmmakers use similar beast-consummation imagery in clever ways. In *Star Wars: Episode IV – A New Hope*, Hans Solo, Luke Skywalker, and Princess Leia find themselves trapped in a waterlogged garbage compactor, being squeezed and nearly devoured by unseen water monsters swimming beneath the surface. They are "in the belly of the whale" and are being eaten by the Beast, which in this case is both the mechanical compactor and the unseen water monsters hiding below the surface. In the novel and film *The Life of Pi*, Pi discovers that the island on which he has found shelter is actually a carnivorous island that has eaten a man before and will eat him if he does not muster the courage to get back on his miserable boat. Each of these scenarios places the hero squarely "in the jaws" of the Beast.

While Jonah is inside the sea serpent, he repents, admits his mistakes, and begs forgiveness, actions which are key to his survival not only in the tale but also in religious literature. Would Jonah have repented, grown, or become a better human if not for the Beast? Had he not been consumed bodily, would he have changed? His repentance is touted as the whole reason his story is included in the three religions' texts, though of course the mythic imagery of the World Journey gives this story generational endurance. After a number of days, God takes pity on Jonah and commands the fish to release him. (Similarly, the huntsman kills the wolf and releases Little Red, George slays the dragon and releases the king's daughter, Luke escapes from the Dianoga in the trash compactor, and Pi frees himself and the Bengal tiger from the carnivorous island.) After he is released, Jonah returns to dry land and does what is considered his moral duty.

———

Mischievous, clever, and protecting. Fearsome and consuming. A guardian and a beast? How can the Serpent be all of these? Our imaginations are ripe with the startling images of snakes, serpents, sea beasts, frogs, crocodiles, and whales, all beastly images of change, and of witches and wolves. The Beast is the all-consuming changer of direction and pivoter of plans.

Now, let's look at the Beast's twin: the Guide.

The Guide

Technically the opposite of the Beast, the Guide will offer the hero something of a reprieve. A helpful guide will often appear from the most unexpected places to steer the seeker through the wild Abyss to emerge strong and successful.

Why would we need a guide? Can't we figure out on our own what we need to do to navigate our way through the World Journey, to fix a difficult situation, to overcome the odds in business and life? Apparently not. A guide is a necessity, not a simple luxury to help along the way but a truly needed companion to support and care for us during times of crisis. It is the very basis of a community or society in which people interact.

The Guide can be a person but isn't always, though he or she is usually clearly identified. In Walt Disney's 1940 film *Pinocchio*, Jiminy Cricket loudly sings, "let your conscience be your guide."[23] "Conscience" is the whistling, smiling mentor who hops from shoulder to pocket and helps Pinocchio on his path to astonishing transformation. In the Greek myth of Persephone (following on the older myth of Inanna), either the goddess Hecate or the wing-footed god Hermes (depending on the version) arrives to physically escort the goddess through the gates to safety. In the Russian

---

23. Sharpsteen and Luske, *Pinocchio.*

folktale "Vasalisa," the girl is helped by a tiny, pocket-size, magic doll given to her by her dying mother; she keeps the doll in her pocket and feeds it scraps of food. In exchange, the doll tells Vasalisa what to say to get out of sticky situations with the witch Baba Yaga, and the doll even does many of the domestic chores for her.

In *The Wizard of Oz*, Dorothy finds several guides. The Lion, the Tin Man, and the Scarecrow all act in this supporting role, helping Dorothy literally find her way through the World Journey locations of Munchkinland, the forest, and Emerald City to get questions answered. Ultimately, the Wicked Witch of the West is the Beast that demands transformation from Dorothy, and Glinda, the Good Witch of the North, is the informative Guide who shows Dorothy how to transport herself back to the world of reality.

J. R. R. Tolkien was fond of the Guide figure, giving his cast of fledgling adventurers several clear guides in *The Hobbit* and *The Lord of the Rings* trilogy. Gandalf emerges as the most obvious (and proves that even guides can be fallible), while Strider (Lord Aragorn) literally saves the lives of Frodo Baggins and Samwise Gamgee and shows them the way forward. In *The Lion, the Witch and the Wardrobe* by C. S. Lewis, Tumnus the faun befriends the protagonist Lucy, helping her find her way through the Abyss of Narnia. Cinderella gets a magical Fairy Godmother and Peter Pan gets Tinkerbell, who is as much an obnoxious trigger as a guide.

One modern film that capitalizes on the image of the Guide is the 1998 film *What Dreams May Come*, directed by Vincent Ward. The lead character Chris (played by Robin Williams) dies and arrives at a heavenlike place where he is supported by no fewer than three guides: his deceased son and daughter plus a tracker, who leads him to Hell to rescue his deceased wife. Each of these guides provides advice, direction, and handholding to help Chris navigate the labyrinthine afterlife to reunite with his family. And while there are plenty of beasts in the Underworld who would destroy him, the real Beast is the soul-crushing idea of being separated from the ones he loves. Without the guides, he would be lost.

Elements of the Guide

There are three important elements of the Guide persona to mention. The first is that the Guide and the Beast may, in fact, be the same person. Sometimes that which is the most painful and difficult is also capable of showing us the way out. In *Beauty and the Beast*, the character named "the Beast" is obviously the challenge but is also sometimes a guide, and Beauty comes to love him.

In *The Life of Pi*, the young man faces the fearsome Bengal tiger, which is the Beast ready to devour him. But when he is finally rescued, the boy recognizes that the tiger was as much a guide to him as a threat and that his survival depended as much on the tiger as on anything else. Poignantly, the reader understands that the Beast and the Guide were, for him, both parts of his own consciousness.

The second element is that there are sometimes false guides. Not all guides are what they seem. And while the Guide is often a protective figure, some do not necessarily move the hero out of danger but sometimes push them further into obstacles to be faced while the Guide (quite happily) provides advice, tips, and support. Consider Hal, the monotone computer in *2001: A Space Odyssey*, the 1968 film directed by Stanley Kubrick. Hal impresses the heroes of the film with his humanlike understanding, his nimble "mind," and even a sense of compassion. They begin to trust him to the extent that they let their guard down, but at a key moment in the film, they realize that Hal is deceiving them. He was not a guide, after all, but actually a villain. This tech-heavy film was not just a wake-up call about the possible dangers of artificial intelligence; it's a warning about where we place our trust and how much of our strength and self-agency we give away. It's one thing to accept the support of a guide and yet another to relinquish all responsibility for growth and learning.

This "false guide" is similar to the trickster, another type of character we meet in literature and in life. The trickster is usually less evil and is simply lazy or mischievous; however, as we will see in the story about Baldr, the trickster Loki manipulates a situation so completely that the hero succumbs to death. Other tricksters include the Navajo Coyote and the southern Br'er Rabbit, who are not guides but are allotted a certain amount of trust until their true nature is revealed. These two tricksters are also masters of mocking order and causing chaos, triggering a new part of a hero's journey.

Finally, there can be true mentorship with a guide, when the role evolves to encompass more than simply showing the way on a map. A sweet example of this is in the 2004 film *The Polar Express*, directed by Robert Zemeckis.

In this story, a train conductor stops for each child and gives him or her the opportunity to come aboard, teaches them lessons, steers the train, serves as an intermediary between the children and Santa, and provides hot chocolate. In this film, there are many guides—including the conductor, the ghost, and each child's fellow passengers, who learn the value of helping each other.

A mentor is someone who helps you connect the dots because they've connected them before, and their assistance makes your journey (and work) much easier and even more meaningful. To this end, we might look at the role of mentors in our own lives and the extent to which we invite mentors to support us (or that we do not), taking the symbolism of story and making it reality. Finding a mentor allows us to ask questions in a safe environment, seek advice, explore and brainstorm ideas, and watch as someone models something before we try it ourselves. Being mentored is a great gift we can give ourselves, allowing our undeveloped selves to crystallize a stronger and more confident form.

Mentoring is also a rewarding two-way street. While we can ask for the assistance of a mentor by reaching out to request that a friend, colleague, or even a stranger serve as a mentor for us personally or professionally, we can also mentor someone else. A mentor can be anyone: a peer of any age; a person in your same profession or someone who works in a different field; or a person who views life from a different perspective and can offer you a fresh look.

In many of these folktales, myths, and films, we see the Guide as a temporary support person who can help the seeker out of a sticky situation, literally serving as a "tracker" to take them from A on the map to B. But in reality, guides can be short-term teachers, or they can become lifelong supporters and friends, and you can choose to be that necessary support for someone else.

———

If these stories, myths, and tales teach us anything, it is that a true Guide is essential to our forward progress and success and that we must surround ourselves with competent support people who truly have our best interests at heart. It is up to us, and part of our process of maturity, to recognize who is a true guide, who is false, and how their help can assist us getting to the next level, literally and figuratively.

After exploring these dual concepts of Descent and Resurrection, Chaos and Void, and Beast and Guide, it's time to dive (figuratively) into the five locations of the World Journey and explore the impact that each location has on how—and whether—the seeker makes it out alive.

PART II
THE LOCATIONS OF THE WORLD JOURNEY

The stories that capture the Hero's Journey describe the stages of enlightenment—the process where a person goes from confusion to clarity. Here, we will explore more than just the stages. We will look at the often-neglected locations where the seeker goes, *where* the adventure happens, the places that shape the story and position the seeker for growth.

To be exact, we will explore five locations that appear in nearly every World Journey: the Cavern, the Deep, the Vessel, the Forest, and the Labyrinth. Using these enchanting, terrifying, and colorful locations in their stories, ancient storytellers and today's authors and screenwriters relate powerful lessons of self-transformation and maturity. We normally don't perceive the underlying meaning in these tales of cauldrons, mighty dragons, and witches in the woods, but the meanings are consistent across cultures, and the stories—and *places*—are as relevant today as they were hundreds or even thousands of years ago.

In the following chapters, we'll tour through each of these locations of the Journey and will enjoy adaptations of these imaginative tales from around the globe.

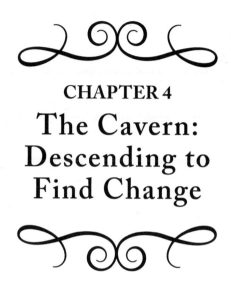

CHAPTER 4

The Cavern: Descending to Find Change

On a chilly December day in 1994, three French cavers cleared away heavy fallen rocks from the opening of what they hoped might be a new network of caverns to explore. They were not disappointed; it turned out to be the massive Chauvet Cave in southern France, one of the world's most spectacular caves containing profound examples of early human art from more than thirty thousand years ago. Its Ice Age art depicts animals—especially woolly rhinos, wild cats, and mammoths—and the artistic beauty is extraordinary. What's more intriguing is that these animals were carefully drawn not on a slate by a fire near the river or in a camp but deep within the most inaccessible reaches of a dark cave. Was there a symbolic significance to this? Perhaps they were drawn as depictions of what the ancient artists had seen that day, or perhaps the drawings were a ritual enacted within the darkness of the cave to influence the hunt and magically increase the number of animals alive in the area—the very first representative imagery. It is fascinating to think of ancient humans crawling through the tight confines of the massive cave, perhaps carrying torches to light their way—into the Abyss—to make art that portrays life. Of these early Paleolithic artists, some say we should "credit them with a pivotal innovation in human history: the invention of symbolic expression."[24] This metaphor—the Cave as womb or birthplace of expression, symbolism, and artistic thought—is the same we find in ancient literature and that we continue to replicate today: the experience of being inside a formless, dark space of nothingness drives expression of form.

Climbing Down into the Underworld

We generally like the idea of rising up. The colorful hot air balloon is the rescue method in *The Wizard of Oz*, the airplane is admirable technology, and the bird (especially the eagle) is a symbol of courage and strength. But the idea of descent terrifies us. Yet, story after story will confirm: the fact that someone can rise up means that they have fallen down in the first place, and venturing into the Cavern is the best example of descent into a dark, scary, transformational place.

For centuries, the Cavern, also depicted as the Underworld, was imagined as a literal realm hidden beneath land or at the bottom of the ocean. The idea that a massive cavern existed under our feet was the basis of many stories, and it has been referred to as the netherworld, Hell, and Hades. The idea of traveling *downward* to reach it is ancient. Our ancestors expected to descend into the Abyss where things are unknown, life is precarious, and survival is all but impossible. To the ancient mind, the interior of the earth was where seeds were sown and bodies were buried. Underground places, such as grottoes, catacombs, graves, caves, and caverns, were especially sacred (and feared) because they were closer to the revered and terrifying Underworld. Countless stories capture this fear and fascination.

Homer wrote his epic *The Odyssey* in about the eighth century BCE, describing the attempt of Odysseus to travel home after his service in the Trojan War. After walking for hundreds of miles, Odysseus is tired, hungry, and lost, so he does what anyone would do: he sacrifices a sheep and pours its blood into an open pit that leads to the Underworld. The pit is the entrance to the Land of the Dead, and when it opens and reveals itself to be a terrifying cavern, Odysseus climbs right in. Once inside, he talks not only with the Prophet of the Dead but also with the soul of his recently

---

24. Walter, "First Artists."

deceased mother, and he is relieved and heartened.[25] He emerges from these conversations into the Upperworld and continues, emotionally strengthened, on his journey.

About eight hundred years later, Virgil writes his epic poem *The Aeneid*, recording the descent to the Underworld by Aeneas. Aeneas is told by a prophet to pluck a "golden bough" from a special tree that will help him survive his ordeal. Together, the prophet and Aeneas journey to a river (the Deep), across which Charon rows the souls of the dead. With the help of his guide, Aeneas will emerge later with the reassuring knowledge of what awaits him in the afterlife.

Soon after Virgil, the stories of Jesus in the early Christian church are written, and vague allusions are made to Jesus descending to Hell/Hades during the three days before his resurrection. Apparently, his purpose was to redeem the souls of Adam and the saints from the cavernous Underworld, who had died long before he could sacrifice himself for them. Interestingly, unlike the other stories, it is made strikingly clear in the scriptures that Jesus was unchanged due to his time in the Underworld—rather than undergoing a transformation himself, he helped transform others.

About thirteen hundred years after that, Dante Alighieri pens *The Divine Comedy* about Dante's travels through the mysterious liminal lands of the nonliving: Hell, purgatory, and Heaven. While in these places, Dante accepts the guide services of *The Aeneid*'s long-dead author, Virgil, as he travels through the Inferno, or Hell. Dante's desire to understand death and resurrection leads him on a terrifying adventure in which both his mind and heart are touched deeply.

In literature, human lives and destinies are created in only a few distinct ways: spinning or weaving, the shaping of clay, and passing through the Underworld. The imagery of the Underworld is a far darker and more foreboding metaphor than weaving threads or shaping clay, as it involves not only life but also death. The image of the Underworld also differs from spinning or shaping clay because it features resurrection, making its theme of life after death shaped by the individual, which is even more inspiring than tales of a life that is spun by gods.

---

25. Seigneuret, *Dictionary of Literary Themes and Motifs*, 365.

Why do so many stories of personal transformation involve going down? Do we ever find stories where the hero goes *up*? Actually, of hundreds of myths, texts, and tales, only a few show ascension first as a means to enlightenment; these include Moses ascending the mountain, Jack climbing the beanstalk, and Hawaii's Hina leaving earth to live on the moon. But these are the exceptions. Generally, stories show a person who is experiencing a shift in consciousness as traveling *downward*, especially down into a dark echoing cave or cavern. Heroines such as Inanna and Persephone crawl through the narrowest of passageways to access dark, remote below-ground caverns where they face their challenges head-on. The descent to the Underworld is one of our favorite and most thrillingly terrifying ideas.

Vegetation Deities and the Resurrection of the Seed

The ground is a very present image. We stand on it daily. It is firm, relatively unyielding, and the holes we dig are dark and littered with rocks and insects. When it does yield to us, the ground opens to reclaim dead bodies. At best, the ground is uncooperative, and at worst, it is a frightening substance. But the opposite is also true. It yields to the most fragile thing: a sapling. Seeds grow from the darkness of the ground, and trees send their roots incredibly deep—who knows what they are touching. The rocky graveyard of our earth produces fruits, vegetables, and grains. It is our first source of life and our final destination.

The life span of a seed was not lost on our ancient ancestors, who recognized that seeds are winnowed, sown in the dirt (underground), remain in the dark for a period of time, and then sprout up again into the light. To reflect this, many ancient goddesses and gods follow a similar path and are today referred to as vegetation gods, meaning that in their stories they are killed, dismembered, buried, put back together, and brought back to life. An example is the Egyptian vegetation god Osiris who is violently dismembered, scattered, and buried only to be reformed and resurrected by the goddess Isis.

Reflecting the stories of the gods, heroes in literature literally journey downward, descending to an underworld where they lose, scatter, or abandon something or where they must fight a monster or perform a difficult task.

The individual then re-emerges (either of their own accord or by being rescued) to the Land of the Living.

To the ancients, the act of descent was a sacred and astonishing journey. Ancient peoples viewed their gods and goddesses as physically making this journey—one impossible for mere mortals—and they rejoiced when their gods and goddesses returned or resurrected. The recounting of a divinity's adventures was the centerpiece of colorful annual rites and festivities. But the journey was also a strong metaphorical image that could not have been lost on ancient peoples; women and men understand at a very fundamental level the symbolism of entering the unconscious (through dreams, trance, meditation, and ritual) to emerge with new ideas, awareness, creativity, artwork, and the perception of wished-for immortality.

Resurrection is a central theme—and it almost always follows harrowing trials. Would these stories have the same impact if someone simply walked down to the cellar and then climbed the steps back up? Of course not. The terror of the Underworld is its treacherous danger. Indeed, *part* of the person must die. The Land of the Dead requires a sacrifice—an exchange for another part emerging. In fairy tales, a young girl (such as Red Riding Hood or Snow White) enters the forest and leaves her innocence there, sacrificing her childish nature to allow her adult nature to emerge. It is a symbolic death of one part of life so another part can flourish.

In the myth of Inanna, the goddess travels downward in a very clear descent past gates where she is challenged repeatedly. When she is underground, the world above is bereft of light and fertility, making this also a seasonal story. Her quest to the dark Underworld is pivotal, for had she traveled upward (to the moon, for example, or to a mountaintop), the story would fail to harness the energy of the fear of darkness and death that is so powerful.

Descent, especially into the earth from which our bodies come, is transformative through resurrection. Ascent by itself, however, especially as seen in religious texts, appears to be permanent—rising into the sky is not an act of a mortal experiencing a personal shift in consciousness. Rather, it is a wholly other experience reserved for the immortals whose ascension indicates everlasting life in the realms of the gods. In the Christian stories, Jesus and Mother Mary ascend; most of us don't expect to see them again. But

Odysseus and Gilgamesh descend first and then rise up—wet and tired but very much human and alive. The fact that these characters rise up again after their grueling experiences is inspiration for us all to persevere.

Thus, our first location for the World Journey is the Cavern. The following two tales of the Underworld portray Descent into the Cavern most graphically: the stories of Inanna and Persephone.

Inanna: The Ultimate Sacrifice

The descent of Inanna and later the descent of Ishtar are Akkadian and Sumerian myths, respectively, that tell the story of the goddess traveling to the Underworld. We'll see multiple popular themes within these two stories: divestiture of personal belongings, trust in a guide, apparent betrayal by a sister (in this case, by the queen of the Underworld Ereshkigal/Allatu), barrenness of the Upperworld, and a miraculous return of the crops with the resurrection of the goddess. The story of Ishtar also includes ritual instructions for anointing the body or statue of the queen's consort, Dumuzi, whose sacrificial descent after Inanna's return leads to the cyclical seasons of the year.

But there are two symbolic acts that truly move the dial on these stories: descent into a cavern and resurrection back out of it. Both stories focus on the descent down from the Land of the Living into the frightening darkness of the cavernous Underworld—and then the emergence from the Underworld having undergone an amazing transformation. In the Akkadian version, Inanna willingly enters the Cavern with a purpose in mind, which is the first indication she is someone to be remembered and why her story has persisted. While descending, she is stripped of everything that is valuable or comforting to her when the gatekeeper tells her "such are the rites of the Mistress of Earth."[26] Quite literally, the guardian of the gate takes her crown, scepter, beads, and every shred of clothing she has so that Inanna enters the cavernous Underworld completely naked and without belongings of any sort. This is her sacrifice—along with the loss of her health and finally her life—because she cannot ascend to live a more meaningful life if she does not leave irrelevant material possessions, such as status symbols,

26. Dalley, *Myths from Mesopotamia*, 156.

behind. With the gatekeeper's extreme demands, we have our first inkling that Inanna is not just traveling down a flight of steps; she is entering a territory from which there is no return: death. Once she's removed her clothing and jewelry and is naked and helpless, she speaks with her sister, Ereshkigal, queen of the dead, who, with a rather dysfunctional family dynamic, tortures her and forces Inanna to endure horrific emotional and physical duress. Eventually she is rescued when her corpse is sprinkled with the waters of life, and she begins the long ascent upward and out of the Cavern of the Underworld. She is allowed to reclaim her life, then her health, and finally her clothing when she emerges presumably as a stronger and wiser goddess.

The imagery makes it clear that Inanna has embarked on the World Journey, has suffered in the Abyss, has achieved some sort of salvation, and has emerged back into the real world. While she has been gone, the people, crops, and animals suffered, but upon her return, they flourish again. On its surface, this is an intriguing story of seasons and cycles, and it also contains elements of cheating (or at least dealing with) death. But upon closer examination, this is a story of humanity looking within, of a single person closing their eyes and peering into the unconscious to acknowledge what truly matters.

NOTE: For simplicity's sake, in the following adaptation,[27] I've woven the primary elements of both Inanna's story and Ishtar's story together. Though Inanna's tale was written first, in approximately 1600 BCE on clay tablets in Sumer, and Ishtar's story was recorded on tablets nearly a thousand years later in Nineveh, they parallel closely with only minor differences.

A STORY: INANNA

The great goddess Inanna decided to visit her sister, Ereshkigal, in the Underworld.

Inanna traveled to the gates of the Underworld, to the frightening Land of No Return, to the abode of darkness, from which none can return. Inanna ventured to the land of dust, of sand, of earth, of

---

27. Dalley, *Myths from Mesopotamia*, 155.

starvation. She arrived at the gate and clearly, loudly, demanded to be admitted or she would break down the door.

The gatekeeper soothed her and reported her words to his queen, the mistress of the earth. But Ereshkigal did not immediately admit Inanna. "Why," she wondered, "would my sister wish to enter? I am the queen of the dead. I am the queen of eternal suffering. It is I who must weep, and I who must cry." Finally, she instructed her gatekeeper to admit Inanna and to bring the queenly goddess before her.

The gatekeeper opened the great groaning door of the Underworld for Inanna, but as she passed through the door, he reached out and removed the great crown from her head.

"Gatekeeper! Why have you taken the great crown from my queenly head?" she asked.

"Welcome, my lady. Because these are the demands of the Mistress of Earth."

Inanna descended to the second gate, but as she passed through the gatekeeper removed the rings from her ears.

"Gatekeeper! Why have you taken the earrings of the queen?" she asked.

"Welcome, my lady. Because these are the demands of the Mistress of Earth."

Inanna descended to the third gate, but as she passed through, the gatekeeper stripped away the beads from her neck.

"Gatekeeper! Why have you taken the lovely necklaces from the neck of the queen?" she asked.

"Welcome, my lady. Because these are the demands of the Mistress of Earth."

Inanna descended to the fourth gate, but as she passed through, the gatekeeper removed the clasps from the cloak about her breast.

"Gatekeeper! Why have you taken the clasps from my queenly cloak?" she asked.

"Welcome, my lady. Because these are the demands of the Mistress of Earth."

Inanna descended to the fifth gate, but as she passed through, the gatekeeper removed the string of gemstones that dangled around her waist.

"Gatekeeper! Why have you taken the jewelry from around my queenly waist?" she asked.

"Welcome, my lady. Because these are the demands of the Mistress of Earth."

Inanna descended to the sixth gate, but as she passed through, the gatekeeper stripped away the bracelets from her wrists and ankles.

"Gatekeeper! Why have you taken the bracelets and charms from my wrists and ankles?" she asked.

"Welcome, my lady. Because these are the demands of the Mistress of Earth."

Inanna descended to the seventh gate, but as she passed through it, the gatekeeper removed clothes from her body.

"Gatekeeper! Why have you taken the very clothes I wear to cover my body?" she asked.

"Welcome, my lady. Because these are the demands of the Mistress of Earth."

Inanna finally stood in the Underworld, utterly naked and without any of the possessions that brought her value or comfort. She greeted her sister, Ereshkigal, but instead of welcoming her, the queen of the Underworld ordered her vizier to infect Inanna with painful and terrible diseases. Inanna was stricken with disease in her eyes, in her arms, in her feet, in her heart, in her head, and in every part of her body. When Inanna was at the peak of her suffering, Ereshkigal took her weakened corpse and hung it from a hook.

When Inanna was sickened, life above her on the earth stopped flourishing. Cows stopped mating. Young men and women ceased in their desire for each other. There was great mourning and gloom, and the hands that once caressed their beloved fell still. Even the gods mourned, and finally the great god Ea fashioned a eunuch to rescue Inanna, believing that the neutral eunuch would not arouse anger or jealousy in Ereshkigal the way Inanna did.

The eunuch did as he was told; he approached and entered the gate of the Underworld and was escorted down through every gate. When he finally stood in the terrible presence of Ereshkigal, the queen of the dead, he asked her for the waterskin so that he might offer Inanna the healing waters of life.

But this enraged Ereshkigal. "How dare you!" she screamed. "No one should ask for such favors." Ereshkigal punished the poor eunuch and cursed him with great misery and hardship. But she did yield and grant his request, ordering her vizier to sprinkle Inanna with the waters of life.

When Inanna revived, Ereshkigal banished her from the Underworld.

At the seventh gate, the gatekeeper returned her clothing.

At the sixth gate, he returned the bracelets and charms for her wrists and ankles.

At the fifth gate, he returned her jewelry for her waist.

At the fourth gate, he returned the clasps for her cloak.

At the third gate, he returned the beads for her neck.

At the second gate, he returned the rings for her ears.

And at the first gate, he returned the great queenly crown for her great queenly head.

But Ereshkigal was not yet done. Fuming, she insisted that Inanna pay her ransom, as no one can simply walk away from the Land of the Dead. "Someone must take her place," she ordered. She sent demons to follow Inanna up through the gates and into the Land of the Living to bring back a sacrifice.

Inanna's beloved partner, Dumuzi, was chosen to be the sacrifice to go to the Underworld instead of Inanna. He was to be worshipped there with great honor, but Geshtinanna, Dumuzi's sister, was heartbroken and cried out, insisting that she take Dumuzi's place for half the year. Thus, Dumuzi and Geshtinanna agreed to trade places every year, and the mating of animals resumed, and the intimacy of people resumed, and in this way does the Great Inanna rule over the seasons of winter and summer.

Here, Inanna's descent into the Underworld is step-by-step, gate-by-gate. When she ascends, she re-establishes the framework of normal life above and guarantees that life and procreation will continue. Inanna returns as if from the womb of the earth itself, naked and reminding us that we cannot take anything with us when we die. We must leave behind clothing, relics of success, and money. To enter the Cavern of the World Journey is to return to something similar to an embryonic state of being—in other words, to a state of *potential* in which we can become anything or anyone at all.

Persephone: A Daughter's Transformation

Written by the sixth century BCE and possibly earlier, the Greek myth of Demeter and Persephone is noticeably similar to the stories of Inanna and Ishtar and can be read with many of the same symbolic interpretations. We have: a great goddess—though in this case, it is the goddess's daughter who descends; Descent into the Cavern of the Underworld; gods who mourn the lost girl and a world that ceases all procreation while she is gone; the return of the girl and the angry call for ransom from the Lord of the Underworld; and the agreement of sacrifice where Persephone consents to return to the Underworld for several months of the year so that the land of the living can have natural seasons of winter and summer with new life.

We also have noticeable transformation; when she finally emerges from the Abyss, she is no longer an innocent weft of a girl, called Kore. Instead, she holds her head high and is now named Persephone, queen of the Underworld and daughter of Demeter. It's a great personal transformation marked by a new identity and even a new name.

———— A STORY: PERSEPHONE ————

In a soft meadow, a girl named Kore and her friends played among the roses, crocuses, violets, and irises. Kore laughed while her mother, Demeter, the great mother of the harvest, watched from a distance.

Kore flitted from flower to flower until she came to a fragrant yellow narcissus, and she reached out her hand to pluck it. But at her touch the ground beneath her feet opened into a great yawning chasm. Kore tumbled into the gaping hole of the earth, and as she screamed, Lord Hades of the Underworld appeared, driving his horse-chariot up to the opening of the chasm and snatching Kore as she fell. He gripped her tightly as Lord of Death and carried her down, down, down through the deepening chasm, away from the light. Innocent Kore plunged downward, into the depths of the earth itself.

From the far end of the meadow, the great Demeter heard her daughter's shriek and rushed to where the girls were playing.

"Where is my daughter?" she cried. "Where is my Kore?"

But Kore had vanished.

Demeter let out a wail of grief, tore her clothing, and pulled her hair. She flew distraught and manic, soaring over the land and the sea seeking her daughter.

She asked the other gods if they saw Kore disappear, but they had been busy receiving sacrifices. She asked mortals, but they were blind. For nine days, Demeter wandered over the earth searching for her daughter. On the tenth day, Hecate, Goddess of Change, Lady of the Threshold, Mistress of Intersections, approached Demeter and said, "I heard your daughter scream, but could not see what became of her."

Demeter flew to Helios and begged him to use his beams of light to pierce the darkness to discover Kore's whereabouts. "What god or mortal man has seized my daughter? Who has taken her against her will?" Helios revealed the truth: it was none other than Zeus, Kore's father, who willingly gave the girl as a bride to his brother of the Underworld, Hades. Helios then chided Demeter for grieving. "Marrying Hades is an honor, and you should be pleased that Hades wants young Kore for his wife," he said.

But Demeter was not pleased; she was enraged and refused to take her place on high Olympus. Instead, she abandoned her queenly clothing and took on the clothing of a peasant woman and wandered through the town of Eleusis, where she sat at a well near several maidens.

"Old mother," they said as they approached her, not recognizing the great goddess. "Do you need help?"

Demeter lied, saying that she had been kidnapped by pirates who had planned to sell her into slavery but she had escaped. "I am old, but

I could be of service. Let me nurse a newborn child," she suggested to them, and the girls immediately hired her as a nurse for their young baby brother. In time, Demeter came to love the baby boy, and she performed a divine ritual to grant the boy immortality. By day, she held the baby against her breast, but by night, she placed him in an enchanted fire and sang divine words over him. One night, however, the baby's mortal mother discovered him in the fire and shrieked, breaking the spell. "Fool!" cried Demeter as she revealed herself to the startled woman as the divine mother of the earth. "Your child would have never aged; he would have been immortal! But now it is ruined." Angry, she told the woman to have her neighbors construct an altar in her honor.

And they did—they built her a beautiful altar—but Demeter continued to grieve for her lost daughter, Kore. In her lasting misery, the queen of grains and cereal caused a dreadful year of suffering for the people on earth: seeds died and famine spread across the land. Zeus did not receive his expected sacrifices, so he demanded that Demeter cease her grieving. But Demeter would not listen. She proclaimed the earth would remain barren and fruitless until she could see her daughter with her own eyes.

Finally, Zeus intervened and sent Hermes down to the Underworld to retrieve Kore. Hermes persuaded Hades to release the girl, but as Kore leaped from her throne, Hades handed her several juicy bloodred pomegranate seeds, delicacies that tempted her since she had been incarcerated in the Land of Death. Kore ate the pomegranate seeds and flew with Hermes up, up, up to the light above and to her mother's temple.

Demeter fell upon her daughter with kisses and embraces, but she suddenly pulled away and demanded, "My dear daughter, assure me that you have not eaten any food while you were below?" When Persephone answered that she nibbled only a few pomegranate seeds, Demeter wailed, for from this time on Persephone was required to dwell part of every year with the Lord of the Underworld, rising from the dark ground every spring and returning, giving the lands winter and summer.

———

There are numerous interpretations of this rich allegorical story. One, of course, explains why we have winter, spring, and summer. It is a straightforward Mother Nature tale of cyclical patterns, and it fits nicely in the vegetation god/goddess category. Also compare Demeter's story with that of Egyptian Isis, who, according to Plutarch's written version, also searches for her missing loved one, poses as an old mortal woman, and places a baby in the fire to confer immortality only to be discovered and revealed as the goddess.

Another interpretation of Persephone's story is the maiden's voyage from girlhood through puberty to womanhood; the girl transitions from innocent maid to womanly queen, and her first menstrual cycle (or her loss of virginity) is alluded to by the red pomegranate seeds. Given the antiquity of this story, likely being sung or spoken hundreds of years before it was finally written as a Homeric Hymn by the sixth century BCE, it was probably a straightforward rite-of-passage story that, over time, lost its focus on maturity and instead highlighted seasonal change. The euphemistic bloodred pomegranate seeds, pushed upon her by her husband, are a lingering testament to what was earlier an overt reference to menstruation, wedding night intercourse, or even rape. The color red has long been used in literature to represent menstruation and especially the end of virginity; consider Little Red Riding Hood's cape, Vasalisa carrying the red embers of the fire, and Sleeping Beauty's needle-pricked finger. For Persephone, the red fruit is symbolic of her violent shift from girlhood to womanhood. Allegorically, as the child must "die" for the adult to surface, Persephone's tale is an intense rite-of-passage story that may have been told by mother to daughter upon her first menstruation to educate the young woman about her new social expectations or to prepare her for (a perhaps bloody) bridal night.

Yet another interpretation is that this is a World Journey story, a tale rich with meaning about self-discovery—an interpretation that in no way diminishes the others. All are valid, and the enduring strength of this story is that it encompasses multiple meanings at once. The story interests me particularly because it shows the descent and transformation of Persephone, but it details the grief, suffering, and duress of her mother, Demeter. Generally in Abyss imagery, the one who descends is the one who works and suffers. This suggests that the personae of the goddess Demeter and her child Persephone are really the same, that they were once considered a unit and have been separated, that the goddess and her daughter are two parts of the same identity much as the Christian God and his son, Jesus, are two parts of the same identity. When we perceive their identities as a unit, both the feminine Greek myth and the masculine Christian scripture reveal a very similar metaphor of descent, suffering, and resurrection.

The Cavern as Death Wish

In addition to the Cavern being a location that supports the transformation of a young woman, as in Persephone, it is used in stories where boys grow into manhood. An example is the 2011 Alister Grierson film *Sanctum*, which follows a dysfunctional father and son with a team of cavers on an egoist adventure to explore the largest cave system ever found. In this story, it is the very frightening nature of an underground cave itself that is the challenge to be overcome, with the hero fighting his own human nature as well as the physical obstacles of the cave. The looping underwater labyrinths become inundated in a flash flood, and the film capitalizes on accidental deaths, merciful murders, unlikely rescues, and general mayhem.

If you've been caving, or spelunking, as it's called, you know that caves are inherently mutable, dangerous, and especially susceptible to weather such as floods. They are so dark that your mind plays tricks on you, you become physically disoriented, and your eyes imagine light that isn't there because it is hard to grasp just how dark a cave can be. In my caving days in graduate school, our outdoor program students visited caves throughout the Appalachian region, donning wool pants and learning about carbide lanterns (but actually using battery-powered headlamps) to explore Grindstaff's, Worley's, and Robert's Caves in the craggy mountains of North Carolina, Virginia, and Tennessee. Worley's is a vast, magical cavern that spans more than 4.5 miles and could easily have been the scene of filming for any number of adventure movies about the World Journey.

Whereas my fellow college students and I learned about the science and biology of the cave, films such as *Sanctum* feature the horrors that can happen in tight, confined, and flood-prone spaces underground, and they instill a sense of nature as destroyer, especially in that film, as the teenage hero takes the powers of nature for granted. In this film, the Beast is two-fold: it is the Cave itself with its sharp turns, flooded passageways, and impossible-to-navigate structures, and it is also the human ego, which is portrayed by people who are overly ambitious and yet tenderly fragile (such as the father and son, who manage to reunite in the end).

The Cavern as Alternate Reality

Instead of looking at caverns as inherent destroyers, some writers view them as opportunities to envision an alternative and intensely creative reality. The earliest published works showing caving as an exciting human adventure come from the mind of French author and "father of science fiction" Jules Verne (second only to Mary Shelley, author of *Frankenstein* published in 1818). Born in 1828 and obsessed with the idea of world travel, Verne was eager to make money through his voluminous writing. He agreed to a publishing contract wherein he would produce three works per year and be paid a flat fee. Already producing adventure works, Verne dove into his new contract wholeheartedly, writing many novels, three of which his publisher termed *Voyages extraordinaires* and which became immediate sensations. This trinity of Abyss-themed science fiction exploded into cultural consciousness at the same time as Lewis Carroll's *Alice in Wonderland*, published in 1865. Verne's trio of books included *Journey to the Center of the Earth* (published in 1864), *Twenty Thousand Leagues Under the Sea* (1870), and *Round the World in 80 Days* (1872). All three became among the most quoted and reprinted stories in the modern era, birthing a new genre of science fiction and an interest in imagining those places that had always been hidden to us (such as the Deep) in innovative and mesmerizing ways.

Journey to the Center of the Earth stems from Verne's idea that tubes must lead downward from volcanoes to the earth's center, which could feasibly be accessed if the tubes were navigated correctly. The story takes a geologist, his reluctant teenage stepson, and their hired guide into an Icelandic volcano where they discover massive and jaw-dropping vistas, flowing mid-earth oceans and rivers of water, ancient animals including live dinosaurs and fish, giant mushrooms, mastodon bones and also a live mastodon, and petrified trees. They also discover a fossilized human and eventually encounter a giant shepherd of the mastodons. After more adventures, the threesome finally "resurrect," exiting the Underworld by ascending up through an erupting volcano that spits them out in Italy. As biographer Tim Ferrant explains, the dangers include storms, ascending a mountain, descending into a crater, and loss of the travelers' water supply, and to Verne's audience, this seemed to be all in a day's work for a scientist.

> *This uncertain itinerary of advances and setbacks, breakthroughs, mistakes and dead-ends, mimics the very business of discovery and disappointment: science ... is made of mistakes which are worth making. The journey is very far from being ... straightforward.*[28]

Verne likens the journey of science to an adventure patterned on the World Journey. Unlike the Cavern as Beast approach, where the innards of the earth are the foe, the novel celebrates the beauty and mystery of what could lie at the center of the earth and guides the reader through an alternate reality that is at once challenging and exhilarating. It's a fantasy vision of what's possible beneath the surface, what is hidden, and what is imaginable, even if it is implausible. It is a search for extremes and for answers, and it celebrates wild imagination.

In 1959 a film adaptation appeared, and in 2008, Eric Brevig's film *Journey to the Center of the Earth* reprised Verne's story with similar themes, with the hero descending into the cavern in search of answers to his missing brother's disappearance. Verne's ideological story inspired countless others, including the children's film *The Goonies* in 1985, where adventurous children discover ships and treasure in the heart of an ancient cavern, and *The Cave* in 2005, which focuses on the unknown hellish beasts that inhabit the Underworld.

---

28. Verne, *Journey to the Center of the Earth; Twenty Thousand Leagues Under the Sea; Round the World in Eighty Days*, xiv.

The Cavern as Hidden Realm of Mind and Spirit

Finally, a seeker may search for answers within the mystical Cavern simply to know, to learn, and to attain inner wisdom. In Tibetan tradition, the hidden lands protect a paradise more illuminating than any text or ceremony, and from this tradition grew the legend of Shangri-La. Veiled in the high Himalayas, nestled between Tibet and India, the labyrinth of Tsangpo Gorge, more than three-times deeper than the Grand Canyon, and its secretive waterfalls, believed to rival Victoria or Niagara Falls, was said to exist. Adventurers lost their lives trying to find it, and it's been wistfully called the Lotus Land and dismissed as fantasy.

Ian Baker's memoir, *The Heart of the World: A Journey to the Last Secret Place*, recounts his years of planning, searching, and failure before finally setting foot in the "elusive sanctuary" and "celestial realm on earth." His purpose as a self-described pilgrim was less to applaud technology (as Jules Verne's novels did) or to conquer nature's obstacles (as Alister Grierson's *Sanctum* characters did). Baker did more to unveil humanity's mistaken perceptions and illuminate where he could. "The Falls of the Tsangpo, one of several portals into this mysterious domain, was not a goal in itself," Baker explains, "but a place of passage, a doorway—whether literal or figurative—to a hidden realm of mind and spirit."[29] This was the ultimate knowing—the result of a journey for wisdom and understanding of nature's mysteries.

Today, the image of Shangri-La implies a paradise of wonder, glorious weather, and problem-free living. The real mystery of the Tibetan Tsangpo Gorge challenges humanity to seek, to press, to explore, and to dream. It fuels the imagination as much as it inspires the real process of climbing, hiking, and trekking. As a location of the World Journey, the Cavern of Tibetan legend is as much about seeking as it is finding.

———

Stories of descent into a dark realm beyond our normal experience—downward into a chasm, cavern, rabbit hole, or well—provide a structure around which our unconscious selves can frame growth. While the big idea

———

29. Ian. *The Heart of the World*, i.

of the Abyss may be a vague and shadowy thought that we can't quite wrap our minds around, the image of a cavern has a shape. And falling down, of course, is easy. The Cavern requires descent and work—and only when the work is achieved satisfactorily can we climb out and return, resurrecting to a consciousness that is stronger, more creative, and happier—with a new identity that signals the completion of our inner work.

CHAPTER 5

The Deep: Into
and Across Water

Our next stop on the World Journey is the Deep. As you might expect, this refers to water—usually an enormous expanse of ocean or a vast sea, a vastness of water so far, so deep, and so uncrossable that it seems impossible that firm ground could exist on the other side. This desperation is exactly what the creators of these myths, texts, and tales want us to feel. The intense stories of the biblical flood and Norse tales of funeral ships being launched out to sea indicate the terror and desperation of people dealing with catastrophe and death.

Reaching back in our minds to the beginning of time is one of the hardest things to do; it's difficult to conceive of the beginning. But to the people of ancient Babylonia, the beginning was very clearly one thing and one thing only: water. Specifically, it was an ocean—a vast, incomprehensible, and seemingly bottomless and boundaryless sea of water for which they had two names: the Deep and Chaos. This formless, fearsome, and watery image anchors their literature and serves as the foundation for many of our ideas of the Abyss.

Deep, Divine Water: The Element of Change

Of all the mutable elements—fire, water, earth, air, and wood—water is by far the strongest element of change, and it resonates with us tangibly. Water in the form of hurricanes demolishes homes, relocates communities, and submerges towns and cities, forcing change with a power we humans can barely face.

In myths, religious texts, and fairy tales, water appears in a similar way as the Cavern—with a form we can envision. It can take on a shape, appearing as a vast lake or the ocean, which, like a cavern, gives our minds something more solid to imagine than a void of nothingness, yet it is still incredibly boundaryless and wild.

Many ancient stories instill water with a persona or character. Often, this was female, and the Deep was frequently called the mother goddess. She expressed both light and dark, life and death; she was the emblem of the past and the prophecy of the future. To those whose very lives depended on the water—especially for fishing and transportation—the ocean was the goddess who allowed it all to happen. She bestowed prosperity and enacted judgment. The Deep was also the goddess who swallowed people whole and wrecked livelihoods.

How can water—or the idea of a goddess—be both healthy and horrible? Myths probably exist to teach us exactly this: that the duality of life is its greatest constant, that life and death are two sides of the same coin. The goddesses Inanna, Ishtar, Isis, and Demeter are figures of abundance and happiness as well as starvation and despair. They are metaphors for the mother who gives birth and the sickle who reaps life. In Nigeria she is Ala, both the creator of the living and queen of the dead. In Ghana she is Asase Yaa, the birther of humanity and the reclaimer of the dead. In Rome she is Ceres, honored for both creating life and for overseeing the death of plants to be eaten as well as overseeing the death of humans and returning their bodies to her sister Tellus Mater, goddess of the earth and soil.[30] Myths tell us that life is *everything* at once, and water is no exception. The ocean gives plentifully, and it takes ruthlessly. Even more important to our thoughts about Descent and Resurrection, the sea is seemingly bottomless and apparently endless, with foreign shores only in the imagination across the distant horizon. This

---

30. Monaghan, *The New Book of Goddesses and Heroines*, 55, 82.

point, above all others, helped form the sea as a symbol of the Abyss, equivalent to the unconscious depths of the human soul.

Water has long been considered both feminine and divine. Salt water—especially the ocean—has frequently been symbolized as a woman and has been given feminine characteristics and names. The earliest recorded examples of this are the stories of the Babylonian goddess Tiamat and the Sumerian goddess Nammu; in roughly 2100 BCE, these goddesses were conflated with the ocean and represented the Great Mother and the Great Deep together.[31] As represented in mythology, water sometimes is male but most often is female. In Chinese traditions, yang (male) energies are dry and hot, while yin (female) energies are cold and wet. In ancient Assyro-Babylonian myth, Apsu was a male god of fresh water, Tiamat the goddess of salt water, and Enki, or Ea, the god of liquid elements (especially rivers and fresh water);[32] Enki's daughter Nanshe was a goddess of springs and canals. Later, in Greek myth, Aphrodite was the goddess of love emerging from the salty sea, and the Deep was a goddess named Thalassa. Still later, in European Celtic myth, Brigit is the goddess of springs.

The Greeks were especially charmed by water's abilities and their myths overflowed with gods and goddesses of water. The earliest seems to be Pontus, whom Gaea produced from her own earthly body at the beginning of time. Next came the impressive Oceanus, a great god with power over every type of water. He shares much in common with the ancient Apsu in that his waters were believed to surround the earth like a river that included the stars. Other Greek mythological creatures associated with water were divided into those of fresh water and those of salt water; salty seas were ravaged by sea monsters, and fresh waters were inhabited by water nymphs. Nymphs were low in the hierarchy of Olympian gods, but mortals adored them and created cults to honor them locally so that every spring, well, still water pond, and brook had its own water nymph who was believed to possess the gift of prophecy and healing. One of the most famous water nymphs was Calypso, who sheltered Odysseus when he was stranded on her island's shores. She hid him for seven years and wanted to keep him forever, but Zeus forbade it.

---

31. Baring and Jules, *The Myth of the Goddess: Evolution of an Image*, 185.
32. Aldington and Ames, *The New Encyclopedia of Mythology*, 61.

Her very name, Calypso, derives from the Greek "to hide" and from the Proto-Indo-European "to cover, conceal, save,"[33] easy images of the Deep.

It is telling to recognize that the Deep was honored precisely because it lacked boundaries. The ocean was not a lake to be skirted or a river to be sailed but a giant body of water so great it defied the imagination. The unpredictable ocean presented a salty and undrinkable liquid, a dark and dangerous nature, and it appeared to harbor monsters. It was of unknown depth, and because its edges disappeared over the horizon—if it even had edges—the infinite sea was considered the ultimate mystery of ancient times. Today we feel we have a certain mastery over the ocean, as we have plied it a bit more with our submarines and robots, and instead we look to outer space as the vast and limitless mystery that defies our understanding. But to the ancients, this breathtaking reverence and awe was reserved for the ocean, and they built their stories of heroes, conquests, and personal growth around it.

Finally, water is considered divine because of its healing qualities; it possesses a miraculous ability to heal the sick and injured. Healing by immersion in water recalls the ancient immersion in the formless, watery depths of the ocean. Romans built their initiation rites, their stage-of-life ceremonies, and their entire concept of spiritual salvation around water, using it to mark many of the most important rites of passage for a human being. They constructed baths and medicinal springs across the region that were devoted to healing and miraculous cures—partly because the water itself was comforting and partly because the deity associated with the well or spring would grant the bather her favor and bring health. Hippocrates waxed eloquent about the healing powers of water, and thermal springs, spas, baths, pools, and wells across what is now Britain and Europe were, for thousands of years, considered curative. This healing quality was part of the reason for their ultimate demise under Christianity (except for their lingering remnant in baptism). With the rise of Christianity, people placed more importance on the masculine qualities of air and dismissed the feminine qualities of water. As a result, previously sacred wells and springs associated with female goddesses and figures became taboo.

---

33. Aldington and Ames, *The New LaRousse Encyclopedia of Mythology*, 146–47, 150; Douglas Harper, "Calypso," Online Etymology Dictionary, accessed March 13, 2015, http://www .etymonline.com/index.php?term=Calypso.

But Romans are relatively new in the line of people who worshipped water as a transformative element. This honor goes much further back—at least to 2000 BCE in the land of Sumer and to the people who called the sea Tiamat.

From Potential to Form: Something from Nothing

The Sumerians founded their civilization on the banks of two mighty rivers, the Tigris and the Euphrates, in what is today Iraq. They associated their gods and goddesses with the Deep, combining the personal characteristics of a god or goddess with the cosmic concepts of potential and consciousness. The Deep was described as a place of limitless possibilities, creativity, and ideas, and it was decidedly female, while its opposite "real world" of structure, achievement, and physical bodies was male. Sumerian literature comprises what are likely our very first recorded stories, and they describe Nammu as a watery mother whose son, Enki, organizes and shapes "the world of men."[34] To the Sumerians, Nammu was the vast and formless female ocean, the Deep, existing in a world of limitless creative potential, who eventually gave birth to a male who brought reason, thought, form, and shape to civilization.

A short time later these ancient stories were enveloped by a nearby and competing group, the Babylonians. We are lucky to have discovered in the nineteenth century seven clay tablets in the ruins of Ashurbanipal's palace library in Nineveh. In an archaeological tale fit for the tabloids, these tablets were translated by a persistent archaeologist named George Smith, who was the first to publish the translations of the fascinating Babylonian story *Enuma Elish*, which tells of the origins of life. In it, the Great Mother goddess Tiamat, like Nammu, is the deep, salty ocean, and she is named Chaos. Later, the Bible introduces Miriam, whose name means "bitter sea" or "salty sea." Tiamat is referred to as "the mother of the deep, the creator of all," while her husband, Apsu, is personified as sweet fresh water and also as the Abyss.[35]

Tiamat: Ancient Mother of the Deep

It is worth exploring Tiamat's story because it is the very foundation of countless myths, religious texts, folktales, and allusions that come later—and

---

34. Grimal and Beardsworth, *Larousse World Mythology*, 58.
35. Harper, *Assyrian and Babylonian Literature*, 283.

because in it we see so many of our current symbols of change, such as oceans, floods, serpents, dragons, rivers, swords, and the duality of dark and light. *The Enuma Elish* tells us that Tiamat lived with Apsu and their child Mummu for eons and that nothing else existed. Finally, their grandchildren are born, and of them, Marduk is the most violent and ambitious. He kills Tiamat and from her body forms the earth, the heavens, and life as we know it.

But this is not only a story of death and violence; it tells of new creation from the Deep because ultimately Tiamat represents potential. She is the muse, conception, and the mother all rolled into one; Marduk represents order and form and is what happens after potential is realized. He is the expression of her idea, and while we may cringe at the seemingly misogynistic wording and regard his actions as extraordinarily violent, it is worth noting that creating form from formlessness can be an earthshaking event. In other words, emerging from the Abyss into consciousness, whether in the discovery of personal identity or in the expression of artistic epiphany, will rattle you, tear you, and utterly re-form your life. It is inherently a violent (though ultimately positive) experience—it is painful and demanding of sacrifice. The emergence of new life is, without doubt, labor.

——— A STORY: TIAMAT ———

The world was peaceful and vague, with light and shadow playing on water and air. The Great Sea Mother, Tiamat, was the goddess of the deep and the mother of the bitter salt waters. She coupled with Apsu, god of fresh rivers, to conceive a child, and soon she birthed the god Mummu, and the three existed as a happy and vague watery trinity. Together they formed the Void, the Deep, and the Abyss. There was no form, no shape, no time. They were the cosmos, a vague and formless place, watery and without land or solid substance. They were made of swirling ideas and liquid thoughts. It was only potential, waiting to burst forth. In this Abyss, anything was possible.

One day, Tiamat birthed more children: silt, soil, and the horizon. From these children were born the sky god, Anu; the earth god, Ea; and more siblings. But the siblings grew loud and obnoxious, and Mummu asked Apsu to kill them to restore the peace. When the siblings learned of this plan, they appealed to Ea, the god of supreme understanding, who was also a powerful magician. But instead of trying to change Apsu's mind, Ea decided to simply lull Apsu into a deep sleep—and he murdered him. Ea stole Apsu's crown and took over his royal power. He built a structure over the underground pool of Apsu. Now the ruler, Ea and his wife, Damkina, created their new home. Ea and Damkina gave birth to Marduk.

Tiamat watched the murder of Apsu, but she did not protest. She was silent, but when an older god visited her and urged her to avenge Apsu's death, Tiamat agreed to retaliate. She pulled forth from her salty, watery depths frightening monsters. She pulled forth dragons, serpents, and ferocious creatures to prepare for battle.

But Marduk was powerful and determined. He took it upon himself to fight Tiamat, confirming himself as supreme ruler with the gods and usurping Ea. He gathered his forces about him and began the great battle against the Deep. Marduk used his element, air, to create powerful winds—the whirlwind and the tornado—to defeat Tiamat's waters and sea serpents.

The watery serpent goddess and the air god fought bitterly, and in the end Marduk won. Marduk didn't just defeat Tiamat. He utterly destroyed her. He trampled upon her neck and cut off her life. Marduk split her carcass in half, creating from it the sky and the earth. With Mother Chaos defeated, with watery Tiamat defeated, with the dragon defeated, with Marduk's airy breath defeating the dragon, the solid world was formed. Marduk was the supreme ruler of the world.

———

During their battle, Tiamat is portrayed as enraged and frenzied, while Marduk is depicted as cool and collected. When Marduk finally unleashes the winds against her, the harrowing poem on the ancient tablets tells us that he created the tempest, the whirlwind, the evil wind, and the tornado. Once he killed and trampled Tiamat, Marduk established the constellations, developed the calendar year, created night and day, and designated days for annual festivals. By creating form from Tiamat's formlessness, Marduk became the hero of his people.[36]

Despite the violent vanquishment of Tiamat, the idea of water as an element of personal transformation tends to resonate much more deeply with us than air. As we'll see in later chapters, water is the key symbol in many World Journey stories from around the world. The cauldron, for example, is an image of transformation prevalent in Irish and Welsh mythology. Water has been the element most associated with the descent of consciousness and connection with divinity—far longer than the element air. In other words, sinking into deep water is historically a more natural symbol of personal growth than ascending into air.

The myth of Tiamat teaches the compelling idea that together with the male energies of aggression and force, slippery, patient water created new life. Water as female potential combines with the breath/air of male energy to turn potential into form and structure—the artistic idea becomes tangible art.

From Potential to Action: Water Is Change

So far, we've looked at shapeless water as potential—an inactive state of this versatile element that can lead to both grounded form and knowledge or wisdom. But water can also be action. For potential to become reality, must it be violent, aggressive, and powerful? Not necessarily, but it does require action. Potential is not energy in motion but energy waiting for motion to begin. It is by its very nature passive, formless and yielding. It is the seeker's actions within the Deep and the act of emerging from the Abyss that create reality from that which is latent and brings form, shape, and growth. It is this metaphor for resurrection that makes the stories of Aphrodite rising from the salty sea or Miriam rising from oppression or Misiti returning to her home in the Ethiopian tale "The Lion's Whisker" (see chapter 7) so inspirational. In water myths—especially the most ancient stories—this metaphor was a flood.

It is impossible to overstate how interconnected the symbols of water, power, motherhood, protection, new life, dangerous dragons, and the tumultuous Abyss are. Water is power is change. Water is death that brings new life. Water is the stuff of life, and yet it takes as quickly as it gives. And the

---

36. Dalley, *Myths from Mesopotamia*, 251–55.

ravages of floods are among the most powerful and transformative acts of change that we humans ever witness; hurricanes and tsunamis have taken lives and changed the landscapes of the earth from Florida to Indonesia countless times just in the last few decades at a scale hard to comprehend and harder to describe. Wrapping up this devastation in the cloak of a story allows the imagery to sink into our minds, giving us symbols that we can pull out when needed to try to relate the incomprehensible. For this reason, Flood stories have been incredibly influential in the development and maturity of human consciousness, and they have been passed down for scores of generations and recorded among many cultures' greatest stories and religious texts.

From Action to Change: The Flood

The Flood. It is an image of unexpected violent action, outright inundation. Chaos. It takes our notion of passive, peaceful water—of the lake beside the house, of the thirst-quenching cup on the table—and creates a monstrosity. Divine, healing water becomes massive devastation.

Literally, a flood destroys houses and villages and takes life—but symbolically, it indicates something much more insidious: the loss of earth, firmament, or anything solid. A flood is unpredictable and unconstrained. It represents a loss of stability and an (unwanted, unbidden) return to limitless potential where anything is possible because there are no rules. Previous forms and structures, such as houses, are wiped away to allow the establishment of fresh, new, and perhaps better forms. For a small village to be swept clear by a flood could indicate potential—perhaps of an eventual fresh start for that town. But for the entire world to be inundated with water? It would mean, symbolically, that *all of life* is an abundance of creative potential waiting to be given shape and structure.

On the deepest level, the Flood forces us to do three simple and yet incredibly difficult things: to examine our desires, to explore our potential, and to act on our creativity. A flood is a catastrophic opportunity to think, plan, and ponder. Emerging from the Deep (as people do in every Flood story) indicates that we have grown and changed in such a way that we will survive.

Nearly every culture on every continent has a Flood myth. Cultural stories of destructive floods are very widespread, leading some historians to suspect that there really was a massive inundation that submerged the greater part of the inhabited world. While this is certainly plausible, we will look at these Flood stories from a symbolic perspective because the wrought emotions and ambitions of humanity surface readily in the words about a flood.

Perhaps most famous is the Bible's story of Noah and the flood, but we see stories of the Great Flood everywhere, even in Central America and Polynesia. There is a story from the Chibcha of Colombia that tells of a god who grew frustrated with humankind and sent a flood. People escaped to the hills and were saved when another god arrived riding on a rainbow. He threw his staff at a nearby mountain, causing it to split in two and drain the flood. Some Flood stories begin with a very specific event that leads to the inundation—such as an earthquake or an erupting volcano in Oceanic mythology. World Flood stories share similar motifs such as mountains, birds, and boats. These images indicate that a person is about to transition from the world of order and reason to the watery chaos of potential.

Ancient Flood Stories: Staying on Top

From ancient Mesopotamia and the Near East, five strikingly similar and horribly violent Flood stories survive:

1. Sumerian, Ziusudra, ca. 2500–1650 BCE

2. Akkadian, Atra-Hasis, ca. 1800 BCE

3. Assyrian Babylonian, Uta-Napishtim, twenty-first century BCE and later

4. Hebrew, Noah, ca. 500 BCE

5. Indian, Matsya Purana, ca. 250–500 CE

The earliest, as early as 2500 BCE but possibly as late as 1650 BCE, is the Sumerian tale of the hero Ziusudra, king of Shuruppuk. Surviving on one single tablet, this story tells how the gods have decided to destroy the human race (created by the goddess Nammu). The god of water, Enki, warns Ziusudra, who builds a boat to "preserve the seed of humanity," climbs aboard, and sails on the raging waters for seven days and seven nights. Humankind is destroyed except for Ziusudra and presumably his family. He is subsequently granted immortality by the other gods and is sent to live in a new and magical land called Dilmun.[37]

Written in approximately 1800 BCE, the Akkadian epic of Atra-Hasis of Shuruppuk tells how the gods have decided to destroy the human race (created by the goddess Mami). Enki warns Atra-Hasis that the water god, Enlil, is planning to destroy the human race, and speaking through a "reed wall," he tells Atra-Hasis to craft a boat. Atra-Hasis builds one and boards with his wife, family, and animals. The world is flooded for seven days, after which Atra-Hasis offers sacrifices to the gods.

An Assyrian-Babylonian story tells of Uta-Napishtim, a resident of Shuruppak, who overhears the sea god, Ea, tell "a reedhut" that the other gods are planning to destroy the human race using a flood of water. Ea tells him to build a vessel, abandon his riches, and flee, taking with him "the seeds of all of life."[38] Uta-Napishtim builds "a great ship," boards with his wife, cattle, and possessions and also with "the animals and birds of the land." A great storm ensues with winds, thunder, lightning, rain, and darkness, continuing for six days and six nights, ending on the seventh day. "All mankind was changed into mud," and Uta-Napishtim wept. His ship lands on the summit of a mountain and Uta-Napishtim releases three birds: first a dove, then a swallow, and last a raven.[39] In this story, Uta-Napishtim and his wife are made immortal and sent to live in the land of "Far-Distant."[40]

Later, the Hebrews record that Noah is told directly by God of his plans to destroy the earth. God tells Noah to build an "ark," to bring two of every living thing into the boat, and that in seven days the rain will begin. Finally, "all the fountains of the great deep burst forth" and rain falls for forty days and nights. God "made a wind blow over the earth, and the waters subsided" (compare to Marduk fighting Tiamat.) The ship lands on a mountain, and Noah releases a dove three times until it does not return. Noah is not made immortal but is instructed to "be fruitful and multiply," insinuating immortality through future generations. He is recorded to have lived 350 years after the flood.[41]

---

37. Grimal and Beardsworth, *Larousse World Mythology*, 62.
38. Aldington and Ames, *The New LaRousse Encyclopedia of Mythology*, 62.
39. Aldington and Ames, *The New LaRousse Encyclopedia of Mythology*, 63.
40. Dalley, *Myths from Mesopotamia*, 150.
41. *The Bible*, Genesis 6:1–9:18.

A similar deluge story comes from India in a Hindu myth where the god Vishnu appears to Matsya as a fish and warns him of an impending flood that will annihilate the world. He instructs Matsya to collect "all higher and lower kinds of herbs and seeds" and all kinds of living beings. He is then to board a great boat that will also carry the seven sages of the world. Vishnu promises to help him during the flood by letting Matsya attach a great serpent to his body that Vishnu can use to drag him to safety.[42]

In 1931 archaeologists discovered compelling substrata evidence of a massive flood in the (real) city of Shuruppuk dating to approximately 3200 to 2900 BCE,[43] suggesting these stories may reference an actual event. Whether or not such a flood is a historically provable event matters little when we look at the great scope of its symbolic effect on generations of people and its ability to evoke the idea of rebirth.

The idea of a catastrophic flood relates to our own lives partly because it may be a historic reality but mostly because it inspired countless stories of traversing the waters of the Deep and coming out on the other side alive. The Flood is a story of survival, of trial and redemption, of inner work and continuation. It is a violent form of Descent and Resurrection, but like the River Styx, which is crossed, the Flood is not a tale of submersion but an image of crossing vast watery depths and staying on top. Images of sailing upon the surface of the Deep during a period of transition (such as from life to death) are ubiquitous in world literature: upon his death, the Norse Baldr is placed on a ship that sails far out to sea; the Mexican Quetzalcoatl resurrects from death and sails across the sea; and the Hawaiian Kaili departs the Land of the Living in a canoe. An obscure Greek myth of pregnant Semele has her imprisoned in a chest and thrown into the sea by her father (see also Osiris); this chest floats across the waters to a distant shore where Semele is dead, but her infant child survives, giving the myth a clear theme of death to the "old you" and rebirth to the "new you." To achieve enlightenment, Gilgamesh traverses the Deep in a boat, and Arthur crosses the waters to pull Excalibur from the hand of the submerged Lady of the Lake.

---

42. The Editors of Encyclopaedia Britannica, "Matsya."
43. Kramer, "Reflections on the Mesopotamian Flood," 18.

The water is the Deep, and crossing it (usually in a boat) evokes the same transformative process as descending into either it or the Cavern. Numerous stories, legends, myths, and actual burial practices involve crossing water, either in death or in life, to access creativity or the "next stage."

Honoring the image of the boat, ancient Norse men and women placed the bodies of their deceased loved ones in special boats, loading them with grave goods and burying the boats as permanent graves. The most famous examples of this are the Viking ship discovered at Oseberg in Norway and the Anglo-Saxon ship buried at Sutton Hoo in England, where the boats may have symbolized the passage of the dead person's spirit across the water. Ancient Egyptians also buried or enclosed boats as part of funerary rites, though, as with the Khufu Ship found in the Giza pyramid complex, they did not place the deceased's body inside. For both cultures, it seems their idea of death involved traversing water, and they provided a ship for the deceased to accomplish this successfully.

Baldr: An Unlucky God

While these ships remained interred in the earth, a few ships seemed to have captured the imagination of the ancient Norse cultures by being set in full sail across the waters, bearing the deceased inside. This practice appears to have been carried out on rare occasions, as most burials staged the scene for the deceased soul to sail over water without actually sending the ship out. But in Scandinavian legends and myths, the idea of sailing across water was an essential element of funeral rites. One such story tells of the Norse god Baldr, the son of Odin and Frigga; the story is replete with images of the Abyss, with magic, with the idea of crossing water via a bridge, and even with serpents that signify transition and immortality.

─────────── A STORY: BALDR ───────────

Everyone loved the beloved and joyful god Baldr. But one day, Baldr began having bad dreams. His father, Odin, and mother, Frigga, grew concerned, so Odin descended into the Underworld to ask the priestess Hel, goddess of the dead, if she could tell him of Baldr's fate. She

answered that she did know of his fate and was, in fact, already pre-
paring a festival to celebrate his pending death.

Devastated, Odin returned from the Underworld and shared the
news with Frigga. Immediately, she asked all the beings of the Upper-
world to promise not to hurt her son Baldr, and to their credit, every
plant, animal, person, and divinity that she asked swore to keep Baldr
safe. In fact, so many creatures promised their love for Baldr that it
became a joke that he could not be harmed, and the gods playfully tossed
sticks and rocks at him and laughed as they simply bounced off Baldr and
fell to the ground.

But Loki, the trickster, tried to stir up trouble. He asked Frigga,
"Truly, have all the beings of the earth sworn the oath?"

"Well," Frigga answered, "I asked all the plants, animals, people,
and divinities . . . except I never asked the mistletoe because it is so
small and innocent, I did not feel the need."

Loki left and soon returned holding an arrow carved from mistle-
toe. He stood beside one of Baldr's brothers who was blind. "Here," he
whispered to the brother. "Pull this bow and arrow, and I'll direct your
arm." Obediently, the brother let loose the arrow and it struck Baldr,
piercing him and killing him instantly.

The world fell into mourning, and Baldr's body was reverently
placed on his massive ship, Hringhorni, and a pyre was built on its deck.
But when the mourners lit the fire and prepared to send the ship out to
sea, they could not budge it, as it was stuck in the sand. Finally, the giant
godlike creature Hyrrokkin appeared riding a massive wolf, holding ser-
pents as reins. She released the ship from the sand, and as it dislodged
and slipped into the water, Baldr's wife, Nanna, wailed piteously and
died on the spot, falling onto the pyre beside her husband. The ship sailed
away in flames, carrying its burning cargo out to sea.

The inconsolable goddess Frigga, in her anguish, asked Baldr's
brother Hermod to journey to the Underworld to plead for Hel to
return Baldr to his life. Hermod descended into nine deep valleys,
finally coming to a bridge over a roaring river. The guardian of the
bridge pressed him with questions and finally allowed him to cross.

Hermod entered the realm of Hel and pleaded with her to let Baldr go. To his surprise, she agreed, but she added a stipulation.

"Only on one important condition," she said. "Every being in the Upperworld must cry in anguish for his return."

Hermod raced back to the Upperworld and relayed the news, and every living being in the land and sky began to weep—except for Loki.

"Let Hel hold what she has!" he screeched, and because the trickster would not cry, Baldr will remain in the Underworld until the end of days, called Ragnarok, when he will finally be resurrected and "reborn."

———

We can readily see the images of the World Journey in this story, but unlike other stories, Baldr's story presents as a tragedy, showing the losses and failures of life and death. The malice of the trickster Loki is blamed for Baldr remaining in the Underworld, but the story ends with Baldr rising at the "end of days" when he ascends from the Underworld to lead with his brothers and the sons of Thor. This is Descent and Resurrection—and a very important reminder that our new purpose is not always what we expect. Our emergence from the Abyss is unique from anyone else's and may not look like success at first and may not be in the time frame we would like.

While the Norse set their boats figuratively or literally adrift to disappear over the curve of the ocean when someone transitioned from life to death, other cultures took to crossing different bodies of water. In Japan, the deceased is believed to cross over the Sanzu River, and the body of the deceased may be decorated with coins to pay for passage. In Greek myth, the Rivers Styx and Acheron were two of the five rivers that flowed around and into the Underworld, forming a boundary that must be crossed by the newly dead. To pay Charon to cross the Acheron or Phlegyas to cross the Styx, relatives would place coins in the deceased's mouth.

In one of the stories of the Great Flood, Uta-Napishtim was granted immortality by the gods and was sent to live in the land of "Far-Distant," across the vast sea. This Noah-like character was later sought out by a character who would become extremely popular in storytelling: Gilgamesh. Let's go into the details of his story to understand just why his journey into the Deep is so compelling.

Gilgamesh: Popular Immortality

Gilgamesh was likely a fictional character, possibly modeled on a real man, whose story became so fabulously popular that it survived thousands of years, beginning originally as an oral tale and later being recorded in cuneiform on stone tablets. After these tablets were discovered in the ruins of ancient Mesopotamia in the nineteenth century, they were translated by archaeologist George Smith, of *Enuma Elish* fame. The adventures of Gilgamesh are seventy-two poems long and take up twelve tablets, many of which are fragmentary and broken but nevertheless provide a nearly complete story. Gilgamesh is the first real quest or adventure story that we know of where a seeker sets off on an adventure to learn something new, and the images of this quest have reappeared in myth and folktale for generations.

Gilgamesh is a common enough man. He is neither wealthy nor immortal, though he is vulgar and shallow. He is a plainspoken fighter who suffers a midlife crisis when his close friend Enkidu dies of an illness. Seeing death take down the healthy and vibrant Enkidu, Gilgamesh suffers the harsh realization that he, too, will die one day—something he has never before considered. He can't bear the thought that one day his body will rot, and this horrifying epiphany jolts him out of his complacent life of fighting, womanizing, and insulting goddesses and sends him out to find an alternative to death.

To appeal to a myth-loving audience, his storytellers reached even further back into time to bring in Uta-Napishtim, the man who survived the flood centuries before and was awarded everlasting life by the gods. Gilgamesh has heard about the famous Uta-Napishtim all his life, and he sets out on his quest to find Uta-Napishtim to learn how he might cheat death.

To find Uta-Napishtim, Gilgamesh travels to the great ocean, the Deep, which is the part of the story we will feature here. After long adventures elsewhere, Gilgamesh finally reaches the shore of the Deep, thinks crossing the water will be easy, and prepares to sail across to meet his Guide face-to-face. But he meets a woman making ale, a barmaid, who stands in his way and warns him:

There has never been a ferry of any kind, Gilgamesh,
And nobody from time immemorial has crossed the sea ...
The crossing is difficult, the way of it very difficult,
And in between are lethal waters which bar the way ahead.
Wherever, then, could you cross the sea, Gilgamesh?
And once you reached the lethal waters, what would you do?
Yet there is, Gilgamesh, a boatman of Uta-Napishtim, Ur-shanabi,
If it is possible, cross with him. If it is impossible, retreat back.[44]

The alewife warns Gilgamesh that the waters are impossible to cross alive. It is an impossible test, she tells him, but Gilgamesh is undeterred. He hires a boatman and makes the crossing, finally meeting Uta-Napishtim and declaring his goal: "Show me how to achieve immortality."

However, Uta-Napishtim doesn't give in so easily, and he proves to be quarrelsome. Instead of willingly helping, he tries to convince Gilgamesh of destiny and teach him that fate has something else in mind for him, not immortality. When Gilgamesh protests, Uta-Napishtim likens death to sleep and tries to explain how impossible achieving immortality is. He proposes a test to prove whether Gilgamesh is worthy of the knowledge: that Gilgamesh keep himself awake for six days and seven nights. Gilgamesh tries his hardest, but being human, he falls asleep. Perhaps Uta-Napishtim wants Gilgamesh to sleep or to meditate in that deep unconscious ground whereby he will understand life's mysteries, but Gilgamesh wakes and cannot go deep enough.

Finally, Uta-Napishtim relents, and as a kindness at the request of his unnamed wife (this story would be a failure without her), he reveals to Gilgamesh that there is a peculiar and magical plant that will confer immortality. It happens to grow at the bottom of the deep sea, where human unconscious will reveal the secrets of life and death. Gilgamesh quickly returns to the boat to sail again across the Deep, and once out in the middle of the sea, he affixes stones to his feet, leaps from the boat, and plunges downward to collect the magical plant. It is a story of questions, of a dangerous descent into deep, dark waters to get answers, and of resurrection—however fleeting—when he

---

44. Dalley, *Myths from Mesopotamia*, 102.

rises with the newfound plant. It tells the desperate and touching story of a man seeking to extend his own feeble life, trying to discover how to matter in a transient and temporary world.

———— A Story: Gilgamesh ————

The great warrior Gilgamesh grieved uncontrollably when his dear friend Enkidu died. In shock, he tore his hair and let his clothing grow sweaty and rank. He would not let his friend be buried for a long, smelly week.

"How can he die?" Gilgamesh wailed. "He has been my friend for years, but now he lies there, unmoving. It is like he is asleep."

He watched over his friend for a week in denial and despair, but then he saw something horrible: a worm wriggled from the corpse's nose and fell out. Gilgamesh was shaken into the realization that Enkidu was actually dead and that he, too, would come to such an end. Gilgamesh begged the gods for answers, but they did not answer him. Bereft, he set out on a great quest to meet the one person who could possibly answer his burning question: Must he, too, die?

Gilgamesh traveled to find the one mortal man who had ever been granted immortality by the gods: Uta-Napishtim, the blessed survivor of the Great Flood. Gilgamesh searched all over the world and finally found Uta-Napishtim's boatman, who was willing to sail with Gilgamesh across the deep and deadly sea to speak to the immortal man. They sailed, and Gilgamesh found Uta-Napishtim on the far shore of the great and distant sea. At last, he asked Uta-Napishtim his question.

Uta-Napishtim answered that yes, like all men, Gilgamesh was destined to die, but he gave him a test. To begin to know if he could ever be made immortal, Gilgamesh needed to stay awake for six days and seven nights.

"A simple test!" cried Gilgamesh, and he agreed, but as soon as he sat down, he fell instantly asleep.

Uta-Napishtim and his wife placed food beside him each day to mark the days he slept. When he awoke, Gilgamesh felt he had only been asleep for a moment.

"No," corrected Uta-Napishtim. "You've been asleep for days on end. Look at the food we put beside you. It's dried out, white, gray, and rotten."

Gilgamesh lost his will and cried out to Uta-Napishtim, "How could I have failed at such a simple task? What can I do? Am I destined to remain mortal and face death?"

Giving up, he turned to leave, so Uta-Napishtim ordered his boatman to provide clean clothes and fresh bathing water for Gilgamesh so he could return home with dignity. Gilgamesh washed and changed his clothes, then he climbed into the boat and the boatman began to row him back across the sea. But then Uta-Napishtim's wife interceded on his behalf and asked Uta-Napishtim to give Gilgamesh something to take back with him. "After all, he worked so hard."

She convinced Uta-Napishtim to give him something for his troubles, so the boatman returned to the shore.

Uta-Napishtim said to Gilgamesh, "I will share a secret with you, a secret of the gods. You will find a plant, a thorny plant that will prick you, at the bottom of the deep."

Gleeful, Gilgamesh instructed the boatman to sail back to the center of the deep and deadly sea. There, Gilgamesh tied heavy stones to his feet and plunged into the water. He sank down, down, down, into the dark depths of the deep. Finally, he touched the bottom of the bottomless sea and reached his hand out—and was cut by a thorn. He rejoiced, knowing this must be the sharp and painful cut of the very plant Uta-Napishtim described. He kicked off the heavy stones and ascended through the water to the surface, carrying the plant of immortality.

Once he was back in the boat, Gilgamesh told the boatman what he had found and that he planned to give some to an elderly person back in his kingdom, to test it and share it among the community, and also to use it himself. He named the plant To Be Young Again.

But Gilgamesh's plans went awry; exhausted, he chose to stop sailing and instead had the boatman pull onto a shoreline where there was fresh water so he could bathe. He lay the plant on the ground but a sly snake wriggled up, smelled the delightful fragrance of the plant, and snatched the plant away. The snake shed its skin and Gilgamesh, too late to stop it, cried out. The snake was born anew and Gilgamesh's chance at immortality stolen forever, his newfound knowledge of life and death small consolation.[45]

———

The story is remarkable because Gilgamesh actively chooses to enter the Abyss and actively emerges from it. While many find themselves participants of the World Journey and do nothing to overcome it or learn from it, Gilgamesh pursues his destiny and succeeds in both entering and emerging. This *action* and his yearning humanity are what make Gilgamesh an attractive hero and has kept this story popular in spoken and written literature for nearly four thousand years. Though immortality is not to be his, Gilgamesh is celebrated for his tenacity and his search for answers.

From Expectation to Enlightenment

Not every hero or heroine emerges from the Journey with the answers he or she was seeking. Take Hans Christian Andersen's story "The Little Mermaid," later adapted by Walt Disney. The seeker, Ariel, lives in the Abyss—specifically in the watery Deep—existing in a state of limbo, unable to do anything on her own or to make anything of herself. Her greatest desire is to emerge, to surface, and to transition from a girl to a woman. But she faces challenges. She must negotiate with Ursula the sea witch or sea monster (the Serpent), agreeing to sacrifice her beautiful voice for her desired change: to be physically transformed, to go from having a mermaid's tail to having human legs. Disney highlighted the romantic idea that she was in love with a prince and needed to become human for him to notice her, though in fact, in Andersen's original 1836 publication, Ariel yearns to live on land not only because she loves the prince but because if transformed into a human, she will gain an everlasting soul, something she lacks as a mermaid. To Andersen, her work in the Deep is about gaining an immortal consciousness in the Christian sense. Ariel's story hails back to the ancient stories of Tiamat, Gilgamesh, and the dragons of the Deep.

---

45. Dalley, *Myths from Mesopotamia*, 119.

Similarly, the 1989 James Cameron film *The Abyss* sets up the characters (and the audience) to believe that the Beast they would be fighting in the depths of the ocean are Russian submarines, and the characters prepare for war. But as the story progresses, it becomes clear that the real Beast is the folly of humanity when one of their own crew develops a murderous psychosis and becomes the true threat. They spend the rest of the film protecting themselves from the danger of their crewmate while ultimately discovering an unknown and friendly species living at the bottom of the Deep. In fact, the quasi-alien species becomes the Guide instead of the Beast, helping the lead character ascend to the top of the water as a hero having averted war. This science-fantasy film has fun with the concepts of the Deep and provides an unexpected twist so that our expectations are challenged in a way that spurs us, as viewers, to look inward.

———

Water is that stormy element of change and a horrifyingly deep element of opportunity. Skimming or descending into water is the symbolic chance for the seeker to look within and face what's needed in the journey to a higher consciousness. It is the process of trans*port*ation, literally moving from one port or shore to another, as well as trans*form*ation, leaving behind an old form and taking the name and shape of a new identity—especially in matters of personal behavior, belief, or sense of purpose.

CHAPTER 6

The Vessel: Resurrection, Reflection, and Rebirth

Water as the Deep and Void, water as the Flood and Chaos...now we look at water as the reflective Vessel that shows us our innermost desires or perhaps a glimpse of our futures. And just because a vessel seems passive and reflective does not mean it is boring; to the contrary, the myths and fairy tales that involve vessels holding precious water—such as cups, chalices, and cauldrons—are among the most enchanting and adventurous stories ever told.

The Shape of Birth and Rebirth

Because the fertile uterus is the vessel of human life, capable of holding a fetus protected by life-giving waters, we extend the metaphor to other objects; to come upon a bowl, goblet, or other vessel in myth, text, and tale is to experience the great regenerative "new life" of the World Journey.

The Vessel makes for some very entertaining stories. We have tales of drinking goblets leading to salvation and of witches' cauldrons brewing soups of immortality, of fish swimming in springs of enlightenment and impish creatures stealing from cooking pots and thieving their ways to higher consciousness. In many ways, the Vessel is a colorful and universal image of life here and life beyond that is so symbolic it is almost taken for granted, but this is only because it is so pervasive. The Vessel surpasses in popularity even the Cavern image of Inanna descending into the realm of the Underworld and the Deep image of Gilgamesh submerging himself in the sea. It is in a vessel, after all, that Cerridwen brews her magic potion of immortality so that she not only can live forever but renew herself constantly. The waters of the Vessel provide the difference between permanence and constant, fresh renewal. The cauldron and its magical watery elixir, especially in Celtic myth, have inspired generations—but other vessels have captured the world's imagination for centuries, including the Holy Grail, the mythical cup from Jesus's Last Supper; the witches' cauldron full of boiling liquid from which Shakespeare's Macbeth glimpses the future; and even Tomie dePaola's enchanting and never-ending pasta pot.

Why does a cup, a bowl, or a cauldron filled with water entice us so much? There is something indefinable about such a familiar image, something mystical about such a common kitchen item. Perhaps it is because to enter the Abyss through the Vessel is to jump into that elusive regenerative chalice and embrace the death-defying and yet common feminine ability to *create*. Like the Serpent, the Vessel is a symbol of both life and death—a vehicle of change and an emblem of sacrifice. Its stories show that success requires strength and split-second decision-making while facing dire consequences. Birth cannot happen without death. This is what the cauldron's myths teach us. Not surprisingly, both the images of the snake and the cauldron—which represent renewal, regeneration, and independent thought—intimidated ancient patriarchal civilizations, who viewed them as showing men's loss of control. To them, these metaphors and stories, including Eve's talking with a serpent and Cerridwen's brewing of a potion, advocated for and proved a woman's potential to achieve independence in her physical and spiritual life ... and it wasn't long before the portrayals were hijacked. What was originally a positive image of a serpent (representing new and everlasting life) was cast as an image of weakness at best and evil at worst. And the originally positive image of a vessel containing life-giving waters was rebranded as a witch's cauldron and marketed as not only frightening but sinfully wicked.

Nevertheless, cauldrons and chalices persist as images of hope simply because we can relate with them. They are common household items. They're so much easier to grasp than the unwieldy shape of the magnificent Deep, which is vague, indefinable, and bottomless. We need tangible symbols, and it helps if we can picture something familiar and that we use in our daily lives. Vessels such as cups, bowls, chalices, mortars, and cauldrons fill this need. These vessels are familiar—and because they hold life-giving water, they have long been associated with the feminine, especially with wombs, just as "the chalice and the blade" distinguishes rather graphically between a woman and a man. From this, we've created fascinating stories that celebrate the transformative properties of the Deep accessible in a simple kettle. Let's explore this third and perhaps most colorfully mystical "location" of the World Journey.

The Vessel as Cauldron

Into the Vessel are poured worlds of meaning. Shaped like a cave—circular, dark, and capable of holding liquid—the cauldron has symbolized birth, rebirth, and lively abundance in cultural stories for centuries, especially Celtic myth. A cauldron is nothing more than a cooking pot—each of us likely has a soup pot in our kitchen right now—but because of a cauldron's round shape and depth and because of its purpose, which is to produce life-giving food, it is an ideal image for immortality. What's more, it's relatively portable. A lake, a mountain spring, and a massive cavern are not things you can take with you when you move, while a cup or a cooking vessel can move with you and be part of your storytelling every night.

Historically, the mythic cauldron appeals to us for two main reasons: it holds abundant and delicious food (or wisdom), and according to ancient myths, it can renew lost life and bring back souls from the dead. Few things are as sacred as a vessel holding life-giving water. The image of the cauldron "combines resonant images of life, death, eternity, and transformation" and encapsulates these great ideas in a neat and tidy package.[46] Beautifully recorded in Celtic tales and folklore, the cauldron supplied abundance and sustenance to an extreme. In fact, it was the source of food or brew that could revive the dead and initiate rebirth, usually for warriors just killed in battle. In what is now Ireland, the god Dagda of Neolithic myth was a male god who represented many things: knowledge, life, death, seasons, agriculture and

---

46. Crosby, *Cauldron of Changes*, 6.

farming, music, magic, and Druidry. He was the chief of warriors who fought on the battlefield, and he possessed a bottomless cooking pot—a heavy cauldron of great abundance that he famously named the Undry. From this pot, Dagda could feed all his people (consider the Hebrew story of Jesus feeding multitudes with loaves and fishes). The cauldron produced an inexhaustible amount of nourishment for all. Another magical cauldron in Welsh literature was named the Pair Dadeni, "the Cauldron of Rebirth." It was a stunning vessel of regeneration in which dead warriors could be brought back to life (to fight again).

The Grimm's German folktale "Sweet Porridge," published in 1812, recalls the magic of cauldrons in a relatable and accessible way: a magic cooking pot produces food…and more food…and more food. In the Grimm's tale, a girl and her mother have nothing to eat, so the girl goes out into the forest where she meets an old woman who already knows about her troubles and gives her a small pot. The woman instructs the girl to tell the pot, "Little pot, cook," and importantly, she also instructs her on how to make it stop cooking by saying, "Little pot, stop!"[47] The pot reliably feeds the girl and her mother, but one day the little girl leaves the house, and in her absence, the mother tells the magic pot to cook. The pot cooks porridge and more porridge and more until the house is filled up and the porridge fills the streets and threatens to take over the entire town. The pot keeps cooking porridge until the girl returns home and says, "Little pot, stop!" American writer and illustrator Tomie dePaola based his children's story *Strega Nona* on this old tale, creating the character Strega Nona (Grandma Witch) and the hapless child Big Anthony. When Strega Nona leaves, she lets Big Anthony look after her house and her magic pasta pot. Having watched Strega Nona make pasta with the magic pot, Anthony has heard her use magic words, and he now tries them on his own:

Bubble bubble pasta pot,
boil me some pasta, nice and hot.
I'm hungry and it's time to sup!
Boil enough pasta to fill me up.[48]

---

47. *Grimm's Fairy Tales*, 184.
48. dePaola, *Strega Nona*.

Big Anthony speaks to the magic pot, and it begins to make pasta, but he doesn't know how to make it stop. It produces more and more pasta, filling up the house and the street and threatening to cover the whole town, but Strega Nona returns and performs the magic rite; she blows three kisses to the pot, and it stops making pasta.

Cerridwen: The Welsh Goddess

Images of soup pots and kitchen cauldrons appear as colorful or whimsical images today, but they were truly an ancient and serious symbol of a magical vessel that had, for centuries, been given powers of sustenance and even immortality by some of the most rural, isolated, and arguably superstitious communities in the world. Probably the most vivid and beloved image of the magic cauldron is found in the myth of Cerridwen, a fantastic Welsh tale replete with imagery of transformation in which Cerridwen is the governess of a delightful cauldron of magic. The name *Cerridwen* can be translated as both "Cauldron of Wisdom" and "Fortress of Wisdom," and the stories about her were compiled by the Welsh Elis Grufydd in the sixteenth century.[49] This tale shows the need for care when guarding a magic pot, and it is a story of good intentions followed by wildly unforeseen results.

––––––––––– A STORY: CERRIDWEN –––––––––––

The beautiful Cerridwen, she of the cauldron, in the land of Wales, lived on a hilly outcrop, and in a great meadow, and deep in the woods, and beside a rushing brook. On a bright morning, Cerridwen birthed two babies: a beautiful daughter and an ugly boy. She was ecstatic for her daughter, but she looked upon the comely face of the boy with sadness, knowing that his days would be full of suffering.

To make his life easier, kind Cerridwen decided to bestow upon the boy the gifts of wisdom and poetry. She pulled out her delightful cauldron, a magical pot in which all the stars of Heaven could be seen. Into this cauldron, Cerridwen poured the waters of wisdom, and she dropped in the leaves, and barks, and flowers, and seeds of 1,001

---

49. Stone, *Ancient Mirrors of Womanhood*, 58.

magical plants. She concocted a simmering, fragrant, enticing brew in the deep Cauldron of Wisdom and Inspiration, and she set it on her crackling fire to cook for a year and a day.

To help her in her work, Cerridwen told her servant, Gwion, to stir the brew for her; he was there in Cerridwen's home, his mouth near the lip of her great cauldron, stirring and guarding the pot as the magic waters bubbled for one year and a day. But when the time came and Cerridwen had looked away for only a moment—the briefest of moments—the waters bubbled and spit, and three hot drops landed on Gwion's finger, stinging him. He immediately put his finger in his mouth and tasted the drops of the magic brew. Instantly Gwion shone with the light of infinite wisdom, gaining all the enchantment Cerridwen had intended for her own son.

Enraged, Cerridwen pounced on the boy, but he turned himself into a rabbit and ran away. Shape-shifting, Cerridwen transformed, too, into a greyhound and gave chase, but when she reached Gwion, he turned into a fish and leaped into the river. Cerridwen changed into an otter and dove into the river, nearly catching him, but he spirited from the water in the shape of a bird. Cerridwen crashed through the water's surface as a hawk and pursued him closely. But then Gwion changed into a grain of corn, falling to the earth where Cerridwen—as a hen—consumed him.

Nine months later, her womb full, Cerridwen gave birth to Gwion, who was now called Taliesin. Cerridwen of the Cauldron could not kill the babe and instead wrapped him in a leather pouch and set him adrift on the salty waters of the sea. Having floated across the expanse of waters, Taliesin became the great poet, the chief of bards, sometimes called Merlin, and wizard guide of King Arthur.

———

This imaginative story has endured centuries because it shows Cerridwen possessing profound magic, including shape-shifting and prophecy. At the same time, she is foolish and quick-tempered—yet kindhearted—and many of us can relate to this. And while author Merlin Stone describes her as a powerful goddess preparing her "Cauldron of the Deep," pouring "the water of prophecy and inspiration" into it,[50] her attempted gifts of immortality and wisdom appeal to those of us who are simple, mortal, and ignorant. How many of us have fantasized about shape-shifting at will, as do the magical Cerridwen and Gwion, avoiding challenges by morphing into something or someone else entirely? The cauldron appeals to common folk because it describes immortality not through the decree of gods but through physical birth and blood—and in a simple cooking pot. Cerridwen is known as the "goddess of the cauldron from which all life flows and to which it returns only to be born again,"[51] and she appeals to all mortal mothers whose wombs generate life and to all parents who wish only the best for their children.

Consider this in relation to the Grail, the chalice famous in the Bible. The cup from which Jesus drank at the Last Supper is an ordinary cup, but he says words over it that suggest the ancient common-man idea of immortality through blood: "This cup which is poured out for you is the new covenant in my blood."[52] It mirrors imagery of regeneration and new life that is present in many tales involving a cup or cauldron. Later, in the Middle Ages, this imagery would be blown up as the Holy Grail to become the primary symbol of a generation of Christians seeking answers to immortality, wisdom, and bloodlines. Yet the Grail, eventually seen as a Christian element, had its source in Celtic mythology. "Originally it was a magic cauldron of which all the gods were envious, and they tried to steal it from one another." Author Pierre Grimal describes an old Welsh poem from *The Book of Taliesin* ("The Sack of Annwn") that tells how Arthur seized the magic cauldron in a dangerous expedition. "The pagan cauldron changed very little when it became the Holy Grail that Joseph of Arimathaea filled with Christ's blood."[53] The Grail would be said to confer knowledge, a miniature version of the ancient Cauldron of Wisdom, which itself is a miniature version of the ancient Deep, stretching back millennia through oral and written tradition to guide humankind to ever-renewing life.

---

50. Stone, *Ancient Mirrors of Womanhood*, 58.
51. Crosby, *Cauldron of Changes*, 47.
52. *The Bible*, Luke 22:20.
53. Grimal and Beardsworth, *Larousse World Mythology*, 351.

The Vessel as Springs and Wells

Though it's not a cup you can lift to your lips, the spring or well is still a chalice-shaped vessel of water. Because it's smaller than the ocean and it's relatively easy to imagine its contours and boundaries, the wellspring became not only a symbol of the Abyss but a very real and sacred place where divinities either lived or visited—and where healing took place. Shrines around the world have been set up inside of or at the entrance to springs and wells, harking back to a time when the Deep was seen as the awesome power of divinity and life. Again, Celtic mythology is replete with images of sacred wells and springs—especially as related to the goddess Brigit. She was the protector and spirit of springs and wells, particularly healing wells and the magical regenerative waters that could restore health to the injured and even life to the dying.[54] Brigit was also the divinity of fire, blacksmithing, and poetic inspiration as well as literature.

Those in ancient Rome loved their wells. Water nymphs were believed to be divine beings who protected people and prophesied the future, a belief that displayed a strong connection to the old ideas of immortality and wisdom. One lovely nymph, Egeria, was changed into a fountain and "foretold the fate of new-born babies."[55] Bubbling fountains, cool springs, and sacred pools were places where citizens could rest, relax, and renew, soaking in waters that invited contemplation and insight. Like the Mesopotamian goddess Ishtar, who with her prophecies and insight into both human nature and human future was called Lady of Vision,[56] the nymphs of these wellsprings were prophetic, and they inspired men and women to look beyond their own natures to address the needs of their families and communities.

Madchen: Meeting Mother Winter

The following story, called "Frau Holle," or "Mother Winter," is not a myth but a folktale, yet it offers clear World Journey imagery that results in the seeker experiencing a descent, a search, and a resurrection. The location is a well, a vessel common and feared in most every country villager's garden.

54. Stone, *Ancient Mirrors of Womanhood*, 64.
55. Aldington and Ames, *The New LaRousse Encyclopedia of Mythology*, 210.
56. Stone, *Ancient Mirrors of Womanhood*, 109.

Imagery of the Vessel, and the Abyss in general, is very strong in children's literature and fairy tales. Most children love to play in holes, to dig, and to splash in water, so it is natural that they easily relate to going downward, playing among the roots of trees, burying something, or jumping into a pool or a well.

A number of folktales use well imagery. Since wells were a common hazard in earlier centuries, many folktales involve the mysteries (and horrors) of children falling or climbing down into a well, often to experience an alternative reality and an adventure. Similar to the story of Vasalisa, who treks through the Forest to reach the hut of Baba Yaga (see chapter 7), is the German story of a girl visiting Frau Holle (Mother Winter) in the Underworld after jumping down a well. The story describes a clear initiatory experience and is also a morality tale ostensibly designed to teach children manners and etiquette. It quite effectively, however, relates the manner in which a person can not only achieve self-discovery and strength (especially integrity) through descent but receive monetary rewards for doing so as well.

The story of this girl hopping down a well and encountering livable new worlds beneath the earth shares traits with Verne's *Journey to the Center of the Earth*, though his novel was published decades after the Brothers Grimm published their oral-history tale in 1812. Collected and recorded by the Grimms and published under the title Mother Hulda in their first book *Children and Household Tales*, the story omits the heroine's name, referring to her as "the girl." We'll call her Madchen, German for *girl*, and we'll give her due place in the lineage of quest stories because it is in her adventure that she grows from a girl to a woman.

——— A STORY: MADCHEN ———

Once upon a time, a young girl named Madchen lived with her stepmother and stepsister. Madchen's stepsister was rude and extremely lazy, and she treated Madchen poorly. Madchen was required to spin every day, and one day, as she sat by the well, she dropped her spindle into the well. Panicking, she ran to tell her stepmother, but her stepmother offered no help. Instead she said, "You must go down into the well to retrieve it."

Terrified, Madchen climbed to the lip of the well and looked down into the dark depths. She could not see the bottom. But she screwed up her courage and jumped in. She fell and fell for what seemed like a long time, and then suddenly she landed—softly—in a grassy meadow. The sun shone and flowers bloomed. Confused, Madchen began to walk, and soon she came to a big stone baker's oven full of bread. The bread cried out to her, "Take us out! Take us out before we burn!" Madchen opened the oven and took out the warm freshly baked loaves of bread and placed one in her apron to take with her. Soon she came to a beautiful tall apple tree that was dripping with bright red fruit. "Pick us! Pick us!" shouted the apples to her. "We are ripe and ready to pick!" Madchen shook the tree and collected all the apples that fell, putting some in her apron to take with her.

Eventually Madchen came to a house where she met a frightening-looking woman. "I am Frau Holle, Mother Winter," the woman said. "Why are you here?"

Madchen told her she was looking for her lost spindle. "Will you help me?" she asked Mother Winter.

"I will," the witch replied, "if you will work for me."

Madchen handed Mother Winter the freshly baked bread and the red apples, and then she crossed the threshold and entered the house where she swept the floor and cleaned. When she completed these tasks, Mother Winter smiled pleasantly.

"There's one more task," said Mother Winter. "You must go upstairs and shake out my feather bed. Shake it hard so the feathers fly! For this is a magic bed, and it will bring fresh snowfall to the lands above in their wintertime."

Madchen did as she was told and shook the feather bed hard. Mother Winter was happy with her and allowed her to stay as long as she desired; eventually, though, Madchen was ready to return home. Mother Winter offered to guide her to her land, and taking her by the hand, she led Madchen to a large door. As the door opened, Madchen was showered with a rain of golden coins, and they stuck to her.

"These gifts shall be yours to reward you for your work," said Mother Winter.

When Mother Winter let go of Madchen's hand and closed the door, Madchen found herself outside her home.

Madchen's stepmother and stepsister immediately saw the gold sticking to her clothing, and they demanded to know where it came from. The stepsister wanted to receive the same golden blessings, so she sat by the well, dropped in her spindle, and jumped in after it. She, too, came to the oven bursting with baked bread.

"Take us out!" cried the bread, but the lazy stepsister ignored them.

She soon came to the apple tree, which shook its branches and called out, "Pick my apples! We are ripe!" But the stepsister ignored them too.

Eventually she arrived at Mother Winter's house and was greeted by Frau Holle herself.

"You must work for me," said Mother Winter, and the stepsister walked empty-handed into the house.

She swept, a little. She cleaned, a little. And when Mother Winter told her to go upstairs to shake the feather bed, she only pretended to shake it. Mother Winter grew weary of the girl's laziness and informed her it was time to leave. She led the stepsister to the magical doorway, and when the door opened, the stepsister looked up, eager to see the golden rain falling. But instead she was covered with black, sticky pitch.

Mother Winter asked her, "Did you expect to gain riches?"

And when she closed the door, the stepsister found herself at her home again. She remained covered in pitch the rest of her days.

———

The well as a type of portal or tunnel down into a netherworld is an enchanting idea. Rather than being filled with water, the well becomes a pathway into a dimension that is both homelike and foreign. In the case of Madchen, the quest is simply to grow up, but she does it with such grace and generosity of spirit that it serves as a morality tale in addition to a rite-of-passage World Journey adventure.

From Potential to Knowledge: Water and Wit

We need form and order in our lives, but water can provide something else we crave: knowledge. The vast, bottomless, shapeless ocean of water that signaled Tiamat's potential changed over time and across cultures to appear in different ways. Specifically in Ireland, the pool of water that represented potential became a little well of wisdom.

The clean, clear waters of the little pool growing at the roots of the hazelnut tree were the home of pink salmon and inspired a delightful tale that entertained generations in the British, Irish, Welsh, and Scottish countrysides. This story draws on two triggers for starting the World Journey: the pursuit of knowledge and the quest for immortality. Note the parallels between this tale and the story of Cerridwen, her cauldron, and Gwion. Here we have water, a tree, and a fish—three of the most powerful images of transformation all together in the same enigmatic story of little Fionn, the boy who stole the wisdom of the world.

─────────────── A STORY: FIONN ───────────────

Young blond Fionn came upon, unexpectedly, a pool of water. It sparkled in the sun off the River Boyne, in the ancient magical days of young Ireland. Surrounding the pool of water were nine tall and gnarly trees: hazelnuts, drifting their thick green leaves over the surface of the water and dropping in ripe hazelnuts from their twisted pods. And in the pool of water, surrounded by nine hazelnut trees, swam a salmon larger and more colorful than any Fionn had ever seen. Fat with eating the magical and sacred hazelnuts, it glimmered with rainbow colors and darted among the shadows of the hazelnut branches.

"You, boy!" Fionn's gaze jerked up from the salmon, and he saw a short red-haired man squatting by the side of the pool. "I am Finn Ecas, Finnegas," the man said to Fionn. At that moment, the man's hand plunged into the water, and when he drew it up, he held none other than the fat magical salmon. He shrieked with delight and thrust the fish at Fionn.

"Here," he demanded, "take this salmon I've finally caught after seven years of trying and roast it hot on that spit for me. But be certain you eat not a speck of it because it contains all the knowledge of the entire world."

Fionn did as he was told and pierced the fish onto the spit and turned it carefully to roast it on all sides. An hour went by and then two, and as the sun set and the fish cooked nicely, Fionn noticed a blister on its side. He reached out to tame the blister but—ouch!—he burned his thumb. He stuck his thumb in his mouth to cool it and felt a whirl of rainbow, sunlight, and wisdom fill him up.

Finnegas looked over at just that moment and saw the wisdom shining out of Fionn's eyes. "I knew it!" he cried. "You are the young Fionn who is destined to gain the vast wisdom of the world, and alas, it is not for me." In anger he chased the boy from the woodlands, but from that day forward, Fionn knew all knowledge there was to know, and he became a great warrior and prophet for his people.

———

It is enough to mention the parallels between this tale and Cerridwen, but also consider the story of Adam and Eve, wherein Eve is instructed not to eat something special because it will confer on her the knowledge of the world. More to the point, we are looking at water and its ability to hold magic, understanding, and change within its slippery bounds. While the pool of water was potential, the act of dipping into its offerings changed that potential to something more pragmatic: wisdom and the ability for a young boy to lead his people.

The Vessel as Cooking Pot and Funerary Urn

Humankind began playing with clay in prehistoric times. The first clay figurines are dated to 28,000 BCE during the late Paleolithic period, long before clay was used to fashion pots. Small figurines resembling women and animals have been discovered in caves in the Czech Republic, and it wasn't for another ten thousand years, roughly, that clay as pottery was developed in China, presumably to craft what may have been bowls. From here, the technology spread to Japan and Russia and ultimately around the world. Pottery was widespread during the Neolithic period, or the New Stone Age, and our agricultural ancestors crafted earthenware bowls, figurines, tiles, bricks, and apparently funerary urns.[57]

What a revelation to contain liquids, such as water, in a vessel! Prior to the ability to craft pottery bowls, our human ancestors had to cup their hands or carve wooden hollows to scoop water from natural wells or depressions in stone. It is helpful enough to contain grains or other firm objects within the confines of a pottery bowl, but to contain water? It is a magnificent turning point in history to fashion a container that can hold life's most mercurial, shimmery element, to craft a vessel where one can gaze on the surface as it reflects light and features, a vessel in which one can cook and provided nourishment and meals, a vessel to sustain life.

But the veil between sustaining the living and honoring the dead has long been thin. To go from cooking in a pot in the kitchen to lying in a very similar pot in a cemetery is uncomfortably close. Just as the revolutionary ceramic pot held nourishment for the living, the common pot has also been used for millennia to hold the remains of the dead, often the incinerated remains post-pyre.

The practice of burning the deceased on a pyre and then placing the cremated remains in a ceramic pot (called an urn) has been recorded for thousands of years, from China to Greece and in other cultures. The ashes would be placed in vase-shaped funerary urns, which would either be displayed or buried in the earth. The burial may be for protection, for the ashes to be closer to the gods, or for the deceased to tap into that liminal sphere of transition. The reasons are no doubt many, differing over time and across cultures, but the urns were without a doubt buried in the earth, pots of clay and bones re-entering from whence they came.

Wasn't this person just cooking with or eating from a vessel by the fire? Now, postmortem, he or she is awaiting the return of life perhaps inside a very similar pot. It's a fascinating turn that Neolithic and Bronze Age people took to the custom of using a pot to house the remains of the deceased when a bubbling soup pot was typically very much a life-giving piece of

---

57. "A Brief History of Ceramics and Glass."

kitchenware. Really, the two pots create an image that is one and the same thanks to their Vessel shape; just as Cerridwen's cauldron or Dagda's mighty Undry contained new life within their walls, so did the funerary ware provide a measure of hope for return. And similar to the ships at Oseberg and Sutton Hoo, the pots with their delicate contents are buried in the ground.

The Vessel as Reflective Seer of Past and Present

J. K. Rowling's use of the Vessel as a pensieve strikes me as quite clever. It's a tool she made up for her Harry Potter series; it is a privately guarded basin in which wizards and witches can store their memories. In practical terms, it's an urn for the undead, a nebulous, swirling cache of memories that are carefully kept safe until one day when they may rise up again. To me, this is a poignant reference to Cerridwen's cauldron of creation and to the Norse Undry, where warriors' souls went to be stirred to life again. Are we not storing memories when we put our loved one's ashes in an urn and place it on the mantel? Isn't the act of thinking, pensively, about our deceased loved ones a practice of recalling their lives? To the ancient women, men, and children who crafted and retold the beloved myths of Cerridwen, perhaps they earnestly hoped their loved ones could return, as easily as a memory, with simply a stir of the magic pot.

The reflective nature of the glass-like surface of water in the Vessel is why it's become such a wonderful metaphor for reflection in general. That is, people use the Vessel to reflect upon their lives and think about their past, or when in myths and tales, they reflect upon what *might* happen in the future. This is the gift of Galadriel's Mirror in J. R. R. Tolkein's Lord of the Rings trilogy in book one, *The Fellowship of the Ring*. Here we are introduced to a magical, wide, shallow silver basin that the elven queen Galadriel stewards in the mythic forest Lothlórien. In Tolkein's book, she invites hobbits Frodo and Sam to gaze into the vessel to see what could happen in the future if their quest fails. They each gaze into the silver basin and are aghast at what they witness, and they resolve to gather their courage and continue their journey. In this way, the reflective nature of the vessel serves as a trigger to not give up and, instead, to persevere.

The Vessel as Mortar

Finally, we come to the image of the Vessel as the mortar. The mortar and pestle have been the hallmarks of pharmacists for centuries. My father is a retired pharmacist, and he keeps a collection of mortars on a shelf in his home, made of a variety of materials including wood, marble, stone, and clay. Each mortar has a matching pestle, the rounded tool used to crush whatever is put into the mortar, whether it be basil for pesto, garlic for tahini, or herbs for medicine. The ancient Egyptian *Ebers Papyrus*, compiled by a scribe in about 1550 BCE, lists nearly nine hundred recipes, spells, and methods for preparing medicines.[58] Many required pounding ingredients in a mortar using a pestle, and this combination tool was likely in use for thousands of years prior to that.

Russia's storytelling traditions have gifted us with the seemingly incongruous image of a giant mortar and pestle being flown in the air by the Slavic or Russian witch Baba Yaga. Is this really on par with Roman water nymphs and Cerridwen's cauldron and perhaps even the funerary urn? Undoubtedly, it is the same image of the Vessel. The bowl of the mortar is, of course, the cauldron (and would come to represent witches and women who work with herbs and spices in general), and in this fearsome and rather cruel tale, it is the traveling vehicle of Baba Yaga, the fierce Grandmother Witch who has the power to grant wishes and change lives, depending on her mood, for better or worse. This colorful tale has a number of variations, but in many of them, Baba Yaga lives alone in a hut that stands on chicken legs (see her story, "Vasalisa," in chapter 7). The hut turns, constantly moving, and the woman herself is both old and young. Her fence is made of bones, and the house can be clean one minute and filthy the next, or there can be a table piled with food one minute and bare cupboards the next. Baba Yaga herself flies not on a broom but in the deep, round bowl of the mortar, and she carries the pestle with her (perhaps a dual male-female image of both chalice and blade).

Together, all these images suggest that Baba Yaga is Chaos herself, the fierce and powerful energy of beginnings and endings, the tumultuous source of life and death. I suspect her imagery is born from a long oral tradition

---

58. "What is the Ebers Papyrus?"

of stories about the Great Mother and that they resemble in many ways the fiery and chaotic characteristics of many early and powerful goddesses, including Tiamat, Ishtar, and Hecate, the goddess of transition.

———

The yielding shape of cups and chalices, of wells and springs, of cauldrons and pots and bowls—these vessels and their ability to hold water, to hold healing teas, to reflect dark and light—these are images of the Abyss as the Vessel. That the bowl or cauldron can both sustain life and claim death and that the Vessel represents not immortality but renewal and return were ancient truths about the Vessel's place in healing, life, and death.

CHAPTER 7

The Forest: Creative Expression and Potential

Perhaps the most enchanting and bewildering phrase in any fairy tale is made of just three small words: *into the woods*. With that seemingly innocent phrase, an entire story takes on new meaning as characters plunge into a very special and threatening World Journey location. Just like falling down a hole, descending into the earth, or diving into the watery Deep, entering the Forest on a quest is a haunting and spectacularly dangerous endeavor. Adults seldom pay it heed, however, since its stories appeal generally to children—thus we primarily see the Forest in fairy tales.

The Forest as the Abyss—as that eerie stretch of existence through which one must travel and face difficulties—is one of the most popular and enduring symbols in all literature. The Forest, or the Woods, is a formless, vast expanse without landmarks and full of leafy darkness, dirt, and dishevelment through which an individual must journey at his or her peril, leaving the safety and comfort—or at least the familiarity—of home. And then, of course, the hero or heroine must travel back—returning to the Land of the Living or to his or her home—to reveal what they have learned, carrying proof of success. These wooded areas are dangerous, dark, and mysterious; the Forest is both Chaos and Void.

The Forest makes for a frightening and harrowing location for personal growth, and children often love to be scared by Halloween play and stories of ghosts, darkness, monsters, and witches. Scary fairy tales are the ideal proving grounds for World Journey imagery, especially that which includes dark forests. Little Red Riding Hood travels through the woods to Grandma's house, Hansel and Gretel travel through the woods to the witch's house, and so do many more. The children are merely walking past trees…yet, while one tree can be a sacred symbol of regeneration, what is an entire forest of trees? It means something else entirely. "Going into the woods" in a fairy tale is an extremely desperate phrase.

Poet Joyce Kilmer wrote that he would "never see a poem lovely as a tree."[59] A tree is poetic because it provides beauty, shade, and food. And though Kilmer may not have intended to remind his readers of the larger-than-life power of trees, the authors of our myths, texts, and tales certainly did. The tree carries tremendous power as a symbol, and it represents a great deal to our unconscious minds: everything from immortal life to a conduit between worlds, from a convenient branch for idling serpents to a barrier across an otherwise open path. From a symbolic point of view, a single "lovely" tree is nothing short of magic.

A Single Tree: Enlightenment

Solitary trees feature widely in myth as sacred and transformative; consider Yggdrasil, the huge sacred World Tree revered in the Norse *Poetic Edda* and *Prose Edda*, often identified as an ash tree. Its branches extend into Heaven, and its three main roots extend deep below the earth's surface into various wellsprings imagined to be filled with holy water. Yggdrasil is said to be the tree from which Odin hanged himself (the gallows tree) and to be connected to nine other worlds, giving this holy tree transcendent meaning. As if Heaven-reaching branches and roots in holy water weren't enough, various creatures live within the branches and trunk of Yggdrasil, including a dragon or snake (the serpent of immortality), which gnaws at the very bottom of the roots where they dip into the holy wells. The other animals present in the tree are an eagle and four stags; this recalls the Central American ceiba tree, a towering sacred World Tree in whose branches the harpy eagle roosts. To the Central Americans, and especially to the Maya, the ceiba became the

---

59. Kilmer, "Trees."

Sacred Tree that extends from the heights of Heaven to the depths of the Underworld.[60]

In Mesopotamia, the Tree of Life was rendered everywhere in artwork, especially notable in the palace of Ashurnasirpal II. To this community, the tree symbolized Inanna, or Ishtar, the mother goddess and the creative fertility of new life. Genesis records two (possibly the same) fruit trees: the Tree of Life, which conferred immortality, and the Tree of the Knowledge of Good and Evil, which brought mortality and death. The serpent tells Eve that though God told her she would die, death was not really the result of eating from that tree. Instead, he told her "your eyes will be opened" and she would achieve the ultimate understanding, like gods, of good and evil.[61] She would discover duality and the meanings of a world of opposites: life and death, male and female, evil and good. Another Tree of Enlightenment, the bodhi tree (*Ficus religiosa*), sheltered Gautama Buddha while he attained spiritual understanding. This tree is associated with legends of regeneration from the trunk and from cuttings and is considered sacred throughout Buddhist tradition.[62]

As we've seen with the Welsh story of Fionn, the common hazelnut tree (*Corylus avellana*) has long been associated with wisdom, and stories such as the tale of Finnegas harvesting salmon from the pool of water beneath the hazelnut tree harken back to a time when magic was felt everywhere. The hazelnut tree's mystical reputation for knowledge and worldly wisdom is even seen in the unrelated but similarly named witch hazel tree (*Hamamelis virginiana*), which grows widely throughout the East Coast of the United States in moist bogs and creeks. Folklore says that its branches can divine the presence of underground water, which is why the Scottish and Irish settlers of the Appalachian Mountains used its slender branches as divining rods for water and for prophecy.

The elder tree (*Sambucus nigra*) has a rich history in European folklore as a home for the Hulda Mutter, or Elder Mother, the great witch who lives within its trunk. Some legends say that the tree must be avoided because it is sacred, while others insist that the tree is useful, though you must ask the

---

60. Jordan, *The Green Mantle*, 242.
61. *Saint Joseph Edition of the New American Bible*, 9.
62. Jordan, *The Green Mantle*, 98, 245.

elder witch for permission before harvesting her edible and medicinal flowers and berries, her leaves that can be used to dress topical wounds, or her bark, which, in folklore, was crafted into musical instruments. The tree developed a reputation for witchcraft in Europe with accusers pointing to a witch in the room by tossing bits of elder bark into a bowl of water and watching how they spun. If the bark tips pointed to a woman, she was branded a witch and prosecuted. Other legends encourage common folk to plant elder trees by their doorways to keep witches away, while still others mention that you can tell a witch because she plants elder trees by her doorway. The May Day celebration of Beltane honors the apple, hawthorn, or birch tree as the Maypole in colorful ceremonies often featuring ribbons, strings, and dancing. In every instance, the individual tree is seen as the embodiment of a (generally feminine) divine source of power.

In China, one story merges the Sacred Tree with the inundation of water. A woman drowned in a great flood and was discovered later to have been turned into a mulberry tree "from whose trunk were coming the cries of a baby."[63] A woman reached into the trunk and discovered the newborn, who rose to great power in society; this is a common metaphor of new birth coming from the Abyss. The traditional religions of Siberia and northern Asia, the ancient cultures of South America's Maya and Aztec, and the native peoples of Australia and New Zealand revered the "World Tree" as a vehicle for transitioning between worlds. It was generally believed in many cultures that the tree's linear directions acted as a bridge between consciousness and reality—between the formless Abyss and the structure of earthly existence.

A Forest of Trees: Transformation Through Chaos

One tree is a metaphor for wisdom or connection between the worlds; a forest of trees is something else entirely. Here we have an image of intense divinity and incredible connections with sources of power, potential, creativity, and wisdom. Where one majestic tree signals enlightenment, a forest of trees signals something much more powerful, dangerous, and arduous. Working one's way through the Forest is the same as journeying through the

---

63. Jordan, *The Green Mantle*, 248.

Cavern, the Deep, and (as we'll discover) the Labyrinth; it is a terrifying trek through the World Journey whose outcome is, if done correctly, success.

To enter the depths of the Forest is to enter the sublime, and poets and lovers have long celebrated this. They have also understood that "sublime" is not necessarily easy or even positive. Today, we tend to cast the woodlands in a positive and enchanted light, referring to forests with a romantic respect and awe and creating beautiful national parks, sylvan trail systems, and places of beauty and respite where families can hang hammocks, picnic at shelters, or hike on well-tended trails. But in most historic literature, the Forest is *not* portrayed as sacred or positive; instead, myths, texts, and tales portray the Forest as—first and foremost—incredibly dangerous.

Especially in medieval Europe, a forest was quite literally a treacherous place full of thievery and violence against those traveling from one distant village to the next, and it aroused well-warranted fear among pilgrims, messengers, and families. Forests in England from the time of William the Conqueror until the 1600s were subject to royal law declaring severe punishment and even death to those who used its resources, including timber, deer, and vegetation, without permission. It was a perilous place that required a certain amount of bravery just to pass through.

The challenges of crossing through a forest, figurative or literal, are many; thievery from robbers may pale beside the more gruesome results of animal attacks. In many cultures, forest-dwelling animals were those whose strength far outmatched that of a human and whose mysterious natures indicated shamanic magic: the wolf, the bear, the eagle, the hawk, the fox, the wild cat. Attacks from these animals were explicit dangers in the crossing of a forest anywhere on the continents of Europe and Asia; hyenas, lions, jackals, and boars awaited the individual journeying through the wildlands of Africa. The terrain of the Forest is unknown and unforeseen; the dark trees conceal chasms, pits, and rivers that can sweep a reckless person to his or her death.

All of this would be reason enough to perceive the dark Forest as one of the five locations of the World Journey, a place where a person walking through can experience a revelatory transcendence to another realm of consciousness. But add to this what many fairy and folktales include: a supernatural person, usually a witch or enchantress (the Beast), who is encountered. On top of all the other challenges, the seeker must ask the advice, permission, or blessing of the most fearsome person in the Forest. On one level, this means the hero or heroine must overcome the fear of the unknown and the external darkness—a dim perception of external forces of reality. On another level, this means the hero or heroine must conquer the fear of that which is already inside him or her, for the Forest represents the internal. Facing your own faults—your own shortcomings—and seeking your own blessings for change and renewal is at the heart of the World Journey, and what better place to achieve this than in the consuming, tangled, shadowy, mighty Forest?

Darkness That Allows for Epiphany

We've explored Chaos and Void as extremes that demand certain nonnegotiable things from the seeker; in addition to these, the World Journey has an extreme trait that makes it an effective symbol of transformation: darkness. More than almost any other image, darkness instills fear in our hearts. We call it various names—uncertainty, confusion, unknowing—and we generally do everything we can to avoid darkness and shine a light on our thoughts and experiences. The mythic Abyss is poised as the ultimate darkness, where light is excluded: the deep sea, a cavern within the earth, a tangled, terrestrial forest. These are very, very dark places. We do not read heroic stories of the World Journey where people sit under a lamp at the kitchen table. Darkness equals mystery, and to not know something prompts questions—which leads one to pursue answers. This pursuit is the beginning of personal growth.

Darkness has long been associated with evil, and the dualities of light and dark have countered each other for millennia. One early frightening image of the Abyss is found in the first book of the Bible. Genesis tells us "the earth was without form, and void; and darkness was upon the face of the deep."[64] By describing the beginnings of the feminine earth as shapeless, void, and dark, the words of Genesis imply that it is meekly waiting to be rescued, which will come in the form of the Word (breath) of God, who says, "Let there be light."

This is in direct contrast to Hecate, who was the Anatolian and Greek goddess of the dark. Often envisioned as the counterpart to Artemis, as Artemis represented the light side of the moon and Hecate the dark, Hecate

---

64. *The Bible.*

is also revered as a sublime goddess of change.[65] She is called the goddess of the threshold, and it is Hecate who is in the doorway when you walk through, moving from one room, existence, realm, or dimension to another. It is she who is in the portal or at the intersection when you are trying to make a decision. Portals present a very exhilarating entry into the Abyss, and savvy authors include them in many modern stories, including Lewis Carroll's *Through the Looking Glass* and C. S. Lewis's *The Lion, the Witch and the Wardrobe*.

Hecate could be said to be the goddess of the portal or even the portal itself. She represents change, and of course change can be a terribly frightening thing. We can't see the future; it is dark. We don't know if our decision will lead to good or cause us the ultimate misery, but it is the act of deciding and moving forward through the doorway that keeps us alive and leads ultimately, even if we must walk through a thousand doorways, to enlightenment. To those who see Hecate as simply the dark part of the moon or the path to death and uncertainty, her fearsome image is one of evil. But for those who see her as the image of change, transcendence, and inner reflection, Hecate symbolizes personal growth. It is by crossing the threshold or entering the portal that a person can create the light of understanding, and this is one of those images that is figurative as well as literal. Walking through one doorway instead of another can literally lead to a different outcome; choosing one building, one job, or one home instead of another can change the direction of your entire life. While the image of Hecate is metaphoric, the idea of opening a door to a new existence can be welcomingly (and frighteningly) real.

Darkness is helpful when one needs the period of reflection and potential that is the Abyss. Are you familiar with the cartoon symbol of a light bulb appearing above a person's head when they have an idea? It's the image of enlightenment, of an idea, of epiphany. But it is meaningless if the area is already light; the light bulb only has proper meaning if there has been, previously, darkness. "Once I knew only darkness and stillness," wrote Helen Keller in her 1903 essay *Optimism*. "My life was without past or future…but a little word from the fingers of another fell into my hand that clutched at

---

65. Stone, *Ancient Mirrors of Womanhood*, 206.

emptiness, and my heart leaped to the rapture of living."[66] The darkness makes any bit of light welcome indeed.

As mentioned, the Void encompasses the dreamworld, a space ruled by darkness. Darkness is the realm of sleep, which is itself a mystery and happens during the night when we are our most vulnerable. The parts of our inner selves that we generally ignore or even fight when we are awake can come to us, unbidden and powerful, when we sleep. Personally, I am a dreamer, meaning that I experience what feels like dozens of dreams nightly, ranging from simple "junk" dreams that I know are nonsense to powerful dreams that seem to carry great meaning. Sometimes wonderful ideas come to me in my dreams, a phenomenon that seems to be experienced by many others who find creativity in their nonwaking hours. We are able to plant magical seeds in the dark, often in the dreamworld, even though our waking minds may not have the time or capacity for great ideas. The dark allows us to do things our waking mind would find distasteful, too difficult, or even impossible; without the harsh light of reality shining on it, an idea seems softer and more acceptable in the dark. Dreams have the option of becoming reality.

Many artists find this to be true. Creating artwork in the harsh light of reality, while making breakfast and washing the coffee pot and getting the kids off to school, can prove quite impossible. Instead, many poets, musicians, songwriters, and artists often retreat to a sanctuary that is quiet and dim, where their ideas may flow freely and the compulsion to look and examine every detail is gone, where both analysis and judgment are held at bay. Alternatively, if a retreat is not available, the artist likely withdraws to a place that is simply mundane; ideas flow freely in the shower or while strolling on a path in the local park. Pulling away from the processes of reality and into the dim recesses where the muse can be accessed is essential to drawing forth the vibrant and uncensored artistic expressions of new things.

The idea of epiphany is yet another way the World Journey works in our lives. Perhaps you've had the experience of enduring a succession of confusing or difficult things throughout a day or week or month only to have a clear idea suddenly crystallize in your mind. You wonder why this epiphany

---

66. Keller, *Optimism, an Essay.*

suddenly happened. It's the result of unconsciously experiencing one of two key aspects of the World Journey: Chaos or Void. These are states of being that allow the mind to shift just enough to leave behind the old way of thinking and to find a new and more successful route. The word *epiphany* comes from the Greek *epiphainein*, meaning "to reveal," and *reveal* comes from the French *reveler* or the Latin *revelare*, meaning "to disclose or unveil." Chaos and Void—states of being that are arguably "in the veil"—work precisely because they are wild and without boundaries. They are a mess. A mess is a fitting image for the symbolic Abyss, literature's ultimate symbol of inspiration.

Darkness That Allows for Safety

Darkness was a pivotal image for the Brothers Grimm. After a childhood and adolescence of intense schooling, studious Jacob and Wilhelm Grimm pursued an interest in folklore and German literature. In 1812, they published a collection of stories they had gathered from friends, families, and historical sources, and over the next few decades they produced grammar books and a dictionary and taught, financially supporting their siblings. Their first edition, *Children's and Household Tales*, was critically dark, both in subject matter (death and violence) and imagery. The stories portray the frightening inside of a wolf's mouth, Rapunzel's isolation in a deep forest, and the witch's oven in "Hansel and Grethel" (its original spelling).

Jacob and Wilhelm published these tales in a strange time; anatomy and physiology were only nascent sciences, and knowledge of the human body relied on a lawless culture where body snatchers dug up buried corpses and sold them to medical students and schools (ironically, another term for these plunderers was *resurrectionists*). Ignorance didn't stop with anatomy. Menstrual cycles were incredibly poorly understood, and few grasped the concepts of paternity or, critically, maternal health, and the role of women in society was generally limited to prostitute, wife, or pauper. While the age of marriage for both men and women rose in Europe during the early nineteenth century, from about twenty to between twenty-five and thirty-three, the Grimm's tales provide a glimpse of problematic, stifling, and dangerous family values and cultural norms.

For children especially (and their poverty-stricken parents), the early nineteenth century was a dark period of abusive child labor. As the Industrial Revolution came to be, small children were increasingly seen as valuable employees due to their size and dexterity—and also because their worried parents had no recourse to demand they were treated properly. In the countryside, children typically started full-time work at just over ten years old, helping with crops and driving horses. In the cities of Britain, the average age to begin work as a chimney sweep, factory worker, or errand boy was only just above eight, and employers were known for abusive treatment. The Factory Act of 1833 and the Mines Act of 1842 prohibited the employment of children younger than nine, but it wasn't until 1878 and the Education Act of 1880 and later amendments that most children stayed in school until age twelve. The times were "dark" in many ways, as both boys and girls were exploited for labor and vulnerable to predatory behavior at every turn.[67]

The Grimm's stories capitalized on the idea of *darkness*, but to their credit, the Grimms highlighted both its frightening and its empowering aspects. In their original collection, the upbeat story "The Poor Maiden" illustrates the refreshingly transformative power of darkness—and not metaphorical darkness but the actual lack of light. In the story, a young orphan girl has nothing to her name but a piece of bread and the clothing she wears. "As she set out on her way,"[68] she encounters hungry children who beg for food and cold children who beg for clothing. The generous girl gives away everything she has except her underclothes, out of modesty, and then she comes to the edge of the deep, dark forest, and she finds even more needy children. "It's pitch black," she reasons with herself. "You can certainly give away your undershirt." So, feeling safe and anonymous in the dark, she removes her last shred of clothing and gives it to a child. Instantly the stars fall from Heaven and turn into silver coins, and she becomes rich. Though the young woman already has the moral integrity to get through life successfully, it is the crushing, pitch-black darkness at the edge of the forest that pushes her that last important bit—allowing her to let go of preconceived limitations and expand her consciousness.

67. Price, "Victorian Child Labor and the Conditions They Worked In"; Editors of Encyclopaedia Britannica, "Factory Act."
68. Zipes, *The Original Folk and Fairy Tales of the Brothers Grimm*, 262.

The Bear Prince: A Beauty and the Beast Tale

Darkness is a theme in the classic tale "Beauty and the Beast," a European folktale wherein a father must give one of his daughters to a frightening beast. His youngest child goes willingly and becomes enamored of the beast and eventually marries him. Swiss folklorist Otto Sutermeister rewrote the Grimm's adaptation of the tale to become *The Bear Prince*, with the beast being a bear of the forest with the requirement that the maiden must keep the house dark at night and therefore not see him.

————— A STORY: THE BEAR PRINCE —————

Long ago, a father raised his three daughters on the edge of a wood. The two eldest daughters were vain, and when their father prepared to leave on a trip and offered to bring them something back, they asked for selfish things. "A pearl," said the eldest. "A blue dress!" said the middle child. But the youngest daughter was kind and simply asked for a single grape to eat.

The father departed on his trip and found a pearl and a dress at the merchant's store. But he could not find a grape. Disheartened, he started to walk home but he ran into a dwarf who asked him why he was upset. "My daughter wants a grape," he said, "but I cannot find one."

"I know where you can find a grape!" replied the dwarf. "At the edge of the forest is a vineyard with a white bear. He will give you a grape."

The father traveled until he found the bear and made his request.

"You can have a grape," said the bear, "as long as you give to me that which first greets you when you return home."

The man agreed and soon arrived home bearing his gifts, but to his sadness, his youngest daughter rushed out of the house to greet him first. Exactly one year later, the white bear appeared at their door.

"What greeted you first?" he asked.

The father answered, "My dog."

The bear was angry. "Give me that which first greeted you."

"It was the apple tree I touched," pleaded the father.

"Keep your promise," said the bear, "or I'll eat you!"

The youngest daughter emerged from the house and reluctantly went away with the bear, traveling deep into the forest. In the middle of the forest was a beautiful castle where the bear and the youngest daughter lived. The bear was kind and generous, and the girl grew to love him, though she did not understand why he had one peculiar rule: there were to be no lights on in the castle at night.

Exactly one year later, the bear took her home to visit her family. After the happy reunion, the father secreted a small box of matches into his daughter's pocket. That night as they went to bed, the girl struck a match to look at her husband in the dark, and she was surprised to see he was no longer a bear but was a handsome young man!

"You've redeemed me," he said. "I was enchanted but now I am free."

———

This story is a simple tale that, like "Beauty and the Beast," showcases several themes typical of fairy tales of the time: selfish sisters or stepsisters, a promise in exchange for a treat, and traveling to the depths of the Forest for a young woman to go through an initiation rite. It also suggests that darkness leads to the realization of true love, showing that love is deeper than what we see in the light or on the surface.

Red and Other Colors: Embers for the Fire

The idea of darkness leads us to think about colors, which are paramount in children's fairy tales and weightier than one would suspect. Despite the fact that colors do not inherently have any meanings, humans have attributed meanings to them since time immemorial—for better or for worse. Colors have long been used in stories to express morals, experiences, and ideas, and this has led to both creativity and misery for much of history. For example, the idea that black represents evil or something sinister and that white symbolizes virginity or innocence is a complete falsehood that impacts actual people in their daily lives, and it's a concept that today's writers and filmmakers must be acutely aware of and must challenge in order to advance ourselves past the nonsense of skin color judgments, inequities, and racism. However, we live with a centuries-old heritage in fairy tales and myths that is founded precisely on a person's color or on the colors around them that serves a symbolic role in the story, and to understand historic tales, we must understand the use of color, even if it is outdated and archaic. In addition to black and white having their own symbolism, purple, for instance, has politically been the color of royalty and yellow the color of jesters and folly. Green can represent nature or naivete, and the color red has a special place in fairy tale, folktale, myth, and even religious texts the world over because it is the color of blood.

The color red is a transformative symbol that indicates a person is going from one stage to another. In children's tales specifically, red blood signifies tremendous change: the passage from innocence to maturity. Blood shed by a male can indicate growth from boyhood to manhood, especially in tales of heroism, but most fairy tales that include blood or simply the color red do so to indicate that a girl is experiencing the most profound and often dangerous change of her life to date—not only from a girl to a woman but often from a girl straight to a wife. Author Joan Gould tells us that fairy tales "illuminate the metamorphoses at each stage of a woman's life: those shifts in consciousness as well as biology that propel women from one level of being to another."[69]

The story "Little Red Riding Hood" is one of the best known examples; in it, an innocent child goes "into the woods" to visit Grandma, but the many symbols in the story confirm that Little Red is really journeying to achieve emotional, spiritual, and physical maturity. Yes, the Forest clues us into the fact that she is entering a place where she must overcome real dangers of robbery or attack to reach her destination—and it is the place of the subconscious where she will find the strength to change—but other images speak to the purpose of her journey, especially the color red and the Beast she encounters along the way.

In fairy tales, images of the World Journey occur on multiple figurative levels, readying girls for the demanding physical transformation of puberty.

---

69. Gould, *Spinning Straw into Gold*, vi.

Many fairy tales appear to be dire warnings to young women for what they can expect in the marriage bed, especially relevant in the not-so-distant past when young girls were frequently wedded to much older men. The earliest recorded Grimm tales show these themes bluntly:

- A princess is shamed into sleeping with a pushy frog who demands to share her bed in exchange for a kindness.
- Little Red undresses and climbs into bed where she is devoured by a wolf—today, "being eaten by the wolf" and "seeing the wolf" are French euphemisms for losing one's virginity.
- Snow White's initiation into adulthood involves cleaning house for seven men.
- Beauty must accept the advances of the huge, hairy Beast and simply trust that she will one day be happy.

Blatant change from virgin to wife is deeply embedded in the imagery of these children's tales, sadly and pragmatically preparing girls for what to expect upon their bridal night.

Sexual maturity is a key point of World Journey imagery in the fairy tale "Rapunzel," where the twelve-year-old girl is brought by the witch into the Forest to live isolated in a sleepy, nebulous state of timelessness in a tower. Alone in the middle of the woods, the girl blossoms into her beauty and attracts the attention of a man; she experiences sexuality and becomes pregnant. "Why are my clothes becoming too tight?" she innocently asks the witch, who immediately understands she is pregnant and expels her from the tower.[70] Rapunzel is banished into yet another wilderness, where she wanders with her child not as maiden but as mother, the second of the maiden-mother-crone stages of life for a woman. She has changed in the Forest from an innocent child to a sexual adult.

Similarly, the innocent girl Snow White flees her home and travels through the Forest where she learns the skills of maturity: in her case, cooking, cleaning, and caring for men. It was no accident that this story was

---

70. Zipes, *The Original Folk and Fairy Tales of the Brothers Grimm*, 38–39.

repeated to young girls whose extremely limited social and career opportunities were confined to domestic servitude; they were being prepared for the inevitable. Nevertheless, though women's options were few in late medieval Europe and in countries around the world, a girl had to mature and transform from a dependent child to a (relatively) independent and capable woman. The fairy tale story of traversing through a dangerous forest and coming out alive reflected how a girl would one day leave her mother and take up residence with her husband's family.

And of course Hansel and Gretel leave their home and are forced to find their way through a dark, winding, mysterious forest where they stumble upon a witch's house of temptation. Here they are tested; according to most versions, the girl resists the temptations, but the boy does not, and he lands himself in the witch's crate where she fattens him up in order to eat him. The image of temptations on the journey is a common one, for—along with outright frightening creatures—we are also presented with very appealing people, ideas, and opportunities that require us to use our judgment to accept or resist them throughout life. A mature sense of judgment indicates that the seeker is close to exiting the Forest and achieving transformation. (In the case of Hansel and Gretel, Gretel ends up saving Hansel and is the heroine of the story.)

The prick of the finger for Sleeping Beauty indicates that she is awakening from a childhood of innocence into an adulthood of sexual maturity. Sleeping Beauty is "pricked," and her blood is drawn; as a teenage virgin she is ripe for what comes next, and her initiation is one of slumber, the deep sleep of the Abyss, the dreamworld in which her conscious mind can catch up with her quickly maturing body. We can presume that when she awakes, she brushes off the clotted blood and moves forward as a woman and wife.

When the color red blazes its way into a story, we know it's a transformational symbol, a ruse that points to change. For Little Red Riding Hood, it's the cape; for Snow White, it's her bloodred lips; for Briar Rose, it's in her very name, since the red flower is emblematic of her blossoming adulthood. For Sleeping Beauty, it is actual blood, pricked from her finger instead of her womb. In every instance, it signals a young woman's rite of passage; her sometimes painful initiation into menstrual bleeding as a woman; or her perhaps-too-early introduction to sexuality in the marriage bed. In "Vasalisa," which is a Russian folktale dripping with colors and symbols of life and death, the color red appears as the red-hot embers of a fire in a cold and isolated house.

Vasalisa: Brushing Past Fear

I must say that the Russian folktale of "Vasalisa" is one of the most symbol-heavy stories shared through the generations. It features a young girl, named Vasalisa, and the strange and haunting witch Baba Yaga; I always found this witch less frightening and more frustrating because she is incredibly unpredictable. There is no constancy with Chaos. The tale features multiple images of the World Journey, including the Forest; the Cauldron (as a mortar); the colors black, white, and red; and the undeniable presence of a guide, all wrapped up in a story about a brave little girl who tells her stepmother what's what.

It begins with several classic fairy tale motifs: the girl is kind, cheerful, and innocent; the girl's mother dies; and the girl is left with a stepmother and two stepsisters. In terms of the World Journey, she is in the Void; she's bored, lonely, and ready for change. Finally, Vasalisa is sent by her stepmother to fetch red-hot coals with which to light the family's fire—in symbolic terms, to achieve sexual maturity and become a woman. Vasalisa must enter the deep, dark Forest and go to the house of Baba Yaga, a witch who makes Vasalisa work hard and tests her relentlessly (recall the gentler story of Mother Winter), giving Vasalisa impossible tasks to complete. But the girl draws up her courage, keeps her integrity, and is honest and hardworking. Vasalisa finally completes the tasks demanded of her by the witch thanks to her guide, a magic doll, who finishes Vasalisa's tasks for her after she has worked herself to exhaustion. Vasalisa is freed and returns home strong, self-assured, and literally carrying the red embers of puberty.

——————— A STORY: VASALISA ———————

Once upon a time, a young girl named Vasalisa lived happily with her mother and father. But when her mother grew sick, Vasalisa leaned into her on her deathbed to receive a parting gift: a small doll. Her mother told her to feed the doll and it would take care of her. Vasalisa secreted the doll in her pocket and continued to care for it even after her mother died and her father remarried.

Vasalisa's stepmother and two jealous stepsisters were cruel and forced Vasalisa to do most of the housework, but she did it cheerfully and without complaining. One windy night, all the candles blew out and even the fire sputtered to a stop. In the dark and cold, the stepmother told Vasalisa to retrieve burning embers to relight the fires, telling her the only place to do this was at Baba Yaga's hut.

Vasalisa carried her doll into the forest; she was frightened by mysterious sights and unexplained riders that passed her in the dark. But she finally arrived in the very heart of the forest, at a strange hut that stood on giant chicken legs. A fence of bones surrounded the hut, and at the top of each post hung a human skull. Vasalisa was terrified, but she knocked at the gate. At once, Baba Yaga the Witch flew toward her in the giant round bowl of a mortar, with a long pestle in her hands, and she hovered beside Vasalisa.

"What do you want?" Baba Yaga demanded.

"I need burning embers to light our fires," replied Vasalisa.

"You must do whatever I tell you, and do it well; if I am satisfied with your work, I will give you embers to take for your fire," said Baba Yaga. "But if you fail, I will eat you for my dinner."

Vasalisa agreed to these terms; she opened the gate and entered Baba Yaga's hut. Baba Yaga proceeded to command Vasalisa to feed her, sweep the house, cook breakfast and dinner and supper, all of which Vasalisa could do. But then she commanded the girl to perform an impossible task: to separate the good corn from the mildewed corn in a barn-sized pile behind her hut. Vasalisa worked very hard but was exhausted, and only when her magic doll finally helped her was the house clean and the corn separated.

Seeing nothing to complain about, Baba Yaga again commanded Vasalisa to feed her, sweep the house, and cook breakfast and dinner and supper, and to perform another impossible task: to separate tiny poppy seeds from grains of dirt in a barn-sized pile behind her hut. Vasalisa worked very hard but was only able to accomplish it all when her magic doll finally helped her.

At last, Baba Yaga allowed Vasalisa to ask her a question, and Vasalisa surprised her with the wisdom of her question.

"How dare you pretend to be wise! Where did you learn such things?" demanded the witch.

Vasalisa answered, "It is because my dear mother blessed me."

At this, Baba Yaga screeched, thrust the burning embers into the girl's apron, and sent her from the hut. Vasalisa and her doll returned home, where Vasalisa's embers burned up the stepmother and stepsisters and they vanished into the dark.[71]

———

There are many versions of this tale, especially with the nasty stepsisters, but none so colorful as this where the witch is so mutable and a tiny doll becomes the mysterious guide. Showing the courage of the girl, it is a true rite-of-passage story that prepares a girl for puberty and also showcases her mother's love.

Misiti: The Courage of a Woman

Not every Forest or fairy tale is for children. Women are past puberty, but a grown woman will still seek change and transformation. Stories can be lessons for anyone who is sad, bereft, disillusioned, or ready to quit because adults need just as much encouragement as children do. At different stages in our lives, we adults can share tales with one another that teach lessons of perseverance and growth.

One such story, set in the forest of Ethiopia, is the African folktale "The Lion's Whisker." A popular tale among married couples, the story relates the courage of a woman to pursue her quest through the forest, face a beast, and emerge with the wisdom to improve her marriage and the determination to make her relationship work. This has become my favorite tale presented in this book, as it features a woman on a quest to seek knowledge, and she achieves transformation without violence or snarky stepsisters, which is all

---

71. Starhawk and Hill, *Circle Round*, 77.

too common in other tales from around the world. Instead, it is a mature pursuit from a tender heart.

— A Story: Misiti and the Lion's Whisker —

There lived a couple in the village who had grown unhappy with each other and lost the spark of their love. Misiti, the wife, loved her husband, but they seemed to have grown apart, and she didn't know what to do. She visited the local elder to ask his advice.

"Before you give up on your marriage," the elder told her, "consider giving your husband a magic potion. I can make it for you, and it will turn your husband's eyes to you in a loving way."

"I will!" Misiti said. "Please make it for me!"

But the elder warned her it was not easy. "In fact, the potion requires a very special ingredient," he said, "that is all but impossible to retrieve: a whisker from the chin of a living lion."

"A lion!" Misiti gasped. "But a lion would eat me if I to tried to approach it!"

She sat on the floor of the elder's hut, bewildered, pondering what lay before her. Finally, she worked up her courage and devised a plan. The next morning, Misiti took a chunk of raw meat and walked deep into the forest. She walked and walked, crossing creeks and climbing wooded hillsides, until she at last came to a clearing where a mighty lion stood lapping water at a brook. Misiti trembled with fear and hid behind a tree. Squeezing her eyes shut, she threw the lump of meat toward the lion. The mighty beast startled, but it did not attack. Instead, it picked up the meat and ate it in one gulp. Misiti crept away, went over the hillsides, crossed the creeks, and returned home.

The next day, Misiti got another lump of meat and trekked deep into the forest to face the lion. Again, after hours of walking, she arrived at the clearing where the lion was lapping water at the brook. Again, she closed her eyes and tossed the meat . . . and again the lion snapped it up in his jaws.

The third morning, Misiti did the same thing, and again the next. By the following week, she didn't squeeze her eyes shut. By the third week, she didn't hide behind the tree. And by the fourth week, Misiti crouched next to the lion as he lapped the water at the brook. This time, while he ate the meat, she reached over and carefully plucked a single whisker from the lion's chin.

She left the forest and returned to the elder, showing him her prize. But instead of taking the whisker and putting it into a potion, the elder looked deeply into Misiti's eyes. "You do not need a magic potion," he told her. "You have proven yourself to be brave, creative, and persistent. You have always been strong, and now you are even stronger. Go home and use these skills to improve your marriage."

Misiti went home and told her husband about her adventures, and together they decided to renew their love for each other, creating a happy home.

———

The Forest is an enchanting location of the World Journey that features everything from the Beast to Chaos to simple support from the caring Guide. Snow White, Red Riding Hood, and Hansel and Gretel all walk "into the woods," either voluntarily or not, to achieve something new. Beauty enters the depths of the forest to wed the beast, and Misiti faces her fear of the lion. Their fate takes each of them into a place that is at once Chaos and Void—lacking paths, road signs, and markers. Even Hansel, who drops breadcrumbs behind him to help him find his way, fails when the birds eat the crumbs, and he is left staring at paths that crisscross hopelessly in the dark woods. Of the dozens of tales collected by Jacob and Wilhelm Grimm, many describe the seeker walking "into the woods" to embark on a terrifying and arduous journey. "Rapunzel," "The Twelve Brothers," "The Three Little Men in the Woods," "Hansel and Gretel," "Little Red Cap," "The Girl without Hands," "The Juniper Tree," "The Six Swans," "Little Snow-White," "The Old Woman in the Woods," and many more heartbreaking and disastrous stories hinge on the hero or heroine being forced to walk deep into the unknown woods, where the world's trees that reach from the earth to the heavens grow. It is at once a beautiful and a heartrending image that turns confusion into clarity and fear into courage.

A single tree shows enlightenment. An entire forest of trees? It is in this verdant mayhem where children and adults must find the clarity and strength to grow.

CHAPTER 8

The Labyrinth: Tangled
Webs of Time and Truth

At last we come to the Labyrinth. This last location of the World Journey echoes the same Chaos and Void as the Cavern, the Deep, the Vessel, and the Forest. It is a powerful and ancient image that has enchanted cultures and featured in literature, especially Hellenistic, since the beginning of recorded story.

To enter a labyrinth is to walk—or to dance—from a beginning point into a maze. If you've ever been to a New Age conference center or a camp or retreat center, you may have seen white stones arranged in a grassy area, sometimes with candles or with flowers. People wander slowly among the stones, following a path—or they may dance or skip or do whatever moves them, so long as they *move*. Some labyrinths are outlined on the ground with rocks, sticks, or paint, while others are made with actual walls that tower over a person's head, much like trees in a forest. Either way, it is the symbolic notion of moving through the Abyss that matters. Traversing the confusing Labyrinth involves leaving the normal, rational world behind and entering both the Void and Chaos. A true labyrinth can be frightening and is designed to test not only your sense of direction but also your memory and your patience. It was first and foremost, in antiquity, designed as a severe test and challenge, though modern installations of labyrinths are often contemplative, grounding, and relaxing.

The Labyrinth: An Ancient Idea

Early on, especially in Greece, labyrinths were highly symbolic installations derived from ancient myths that explored many ideas of culture and civilization, including the sacred rite of marriage (*hieros gamos*), the conqueror and the conquered, the appeasement of the gods through sacrifice, and public entertainment. Today the labyrinth is especially appealing as modern societies work to determine the purpose of individual and collective life; artists of opera, games, novels, ballet, film, poetry, music, and concerts have long used the image. With the image of the labyrinth, their artwork pierces our collective idea of the search for the meaning of life. Often this search is more poignant and effective when explored through art, a medium that readily accesses the creative Abyss and its path to epiphany.

By the time labyrinths were popular on sunny Mediterranean islands, the image of the labyrinth was already ancient. "The shape of the labyrinth is already familiar from the Paleolithic and Neolithic drawings of the meander," say Baring and Cashford, "symbolizing the waters beneath the earth, also imagined as a serpent, and referring to the dimension of the other world."[72] The image goes back perhaps tens of thousands of years to cave art where labyrinthine patterns have been discovered. The "meander," as Baring and Cashford call it, was long associated with alternative states of reality and especially with the Underworld. It served a similar purpose as the Sacred Tree, joining together disparate dimensions in harmony. An example of a meandering symbol has also been discovered at Ireland's Newgrange, an ancient stone passageway adorned with twisting carvings of a maze. The irony was not lost on me when I visited Newgrange and saw the fluid, meandering symbol carved into stone for perpetuity—an image of fluidity still solidly present more than five thousand years later. Perhaps carved or otherwise created as symbolic of the World Journey, a labyrinth may suggest the ability to access divine states and emerge as one reborn.

---

72. Baring and Cashford, *The Myth of the Goddess*, 135.

It seems that slowly walking through the maze, quietly pondering life's meaning, was not the earliest way to use a labyrinth. In fact, some scholars suggest that people ritually danced through it. "Dance, in all early cultures, was a way of communicating with the goddess," say Baring and Cashford, "drawing her through ritual and ecstatic gesture into the midst of the spiraling forms that became, as they were danced, her epiphany."[73] Both men and women used the image of the labyrinth to attain ecstatic states of higher consciousness, to reach an awareness beyond that which is normally experienced. The location of the World Journey as the Labyrinth is the ritual and ecstatic awakening of understanding and the revelation of truth.

Theseus and the Minotaur

Probably the most well-known Labyrinth story is the Greek myth of the Minotaur. Very popular throughout Greek civilization, the story is one of war, passion between mortals and gods, deception, and sexual indiscretion—even sex between a woman and a bull. The result of this union was a monster—a human born with the head and tail of a bull. The creature was called the Bull of Minos, or the Minotaur. The king promptly hid him from view in the depths of a vast underground labyrinth that he had built specifically to keep the Minotaur captive, and innocent humans were sacrificed to feed him.

The story that grew from this bizarre conception tells of two heroes: Theseus, the valiant prince who is credited with slaying the monster, and the clever Ariadne, who, thanks to the inventor Dedalus, provides Theseus with a ball of thread, telling him to unwind the thread behind him as he works his way through the labyrinth so that he can find his way back out. The Abyss imagery in this story is classic: it includes plunging into a hazy, vague, and formless underground arena (Descent into the Void); the presence of both a Beast, who tests and challenges the hero both physically and mentally, and a helpful Guide (Ariadne); the emergence out of the Underworld and back into reality (Resurrection); and the shift in consciousness or livelihood of the hero after emerging from the Abyss (self-awareness, self-empowerment, and/or epiphany).

---

73. Baring and Cashford, *The Myth of the Goddess*, 136.

— A Story: Theseus and the Minotaur —

Poseidon, king of the sea, told Minos, king of Knossos, to slay the beautiful white bull he sent him, to prove that Minos was grateful. Such was the way of the gods to demand sacrifices to themselves. But Minos found the white bull too beautiful, and instead of slaying him, he killed one of his own bulls as a sacrifice.

But when Poseidon saw that the white bull still lived and that he would not get his sacrifice, he sought revenge. The god caused Minos's wife, Pasiphae, to fall in love with the creature. Stricken with the curse, Pasiphae asked the craftsman Daedelus to construct a massive hollow cow so that she could climb inside and make love to the bull. Of course her union was disastrous, and she gave birth to a monster. The babe was born with the body of a boy but the head and tail of a bull. Called the Minotaur, he grew into an unruly and abusive beast, and Minos had him imprisoned in a giant labyrinth.

But the Minotaur was constantly hungry, so terrified villagers kidnapped boys and girls from Athens and sent them to the Minotaur for his dinner. Finally, Theseus, an Athenian himself, volunteered to kill the beast. When he appeared at the entrance of the labyrinth, Minos's own daughter Ariadne took one look at him and fell in love. She stopped him before he could blindly enter and handed him a ball of thread.

"Drape this loosely," she told him, "and let it fall on the path behind you. This way you will be able to find your way out of the maze."

Theseus promised to take her with him if and when he returned, and he dove into the labyrinth to face the dreaded Minotaur.

While Ariadne waited, Theseus braved the circuitous ripples of the labyrinth, turning and twisting in mazes that confounded the mind, letting the string fall behind him as Ariadne had instructed. Finally, he slew the Minotaur with his sword, picked up the thread, and followed it back out to emerge victorious. He took Ariadne with him, packing her on to his ship to sail back to his father, King Aegeus, who waited for word of his survival. But Theseus lied to Ariadne, and he abandoned her on the island of Naxos. Yet, in his hurry to leave, he neglected to lift the white sails of victory on his ship, leaving black sails in their place. King Aegeus, watching from his palace, expected to see white sails that would indicate Theseus had won the battle against the monster. Upon seeing black sails, he assumed his son had died, and he committed suicide, plunging into what is now the Aegean Sea.

———

The meanings of this tale are multiple, and the story is rife with allusions and interpretations, which makes it such an enduring (and ghastly) tale. One of the interpretations, of course, is literal—a monster lives in a maze and a hero kills him. Other interpretations require an acceptance of allegory so their meanings can cross the rational plane of our minds and resonate with our inner consciousness, which, of course, is the entire point of poetry and myth.

In this tale, for example, one meaning that is clear to writers Baring and Cashford is that complex sacred marriage rituals were held at Knossos and featured bull-cow imagery with regular sacrifices made to the king. The joining of bull and cow reflected the vegetation god (male) merging with the creative impetus (female), ensuring the continuation of life and civilization.[74] This calls to mind the formless void of potential (woman) joining with the rational form-giver (man) to create life.

And yet another meaning from the story is that of the World Journey, of entering an underground dimension separate from normal reality in which nothing is familiar and danger is pressing. Why would anyone enter such a place? Because complacency leads to death, and the human spirit strives to learn and change. Our inner selves relate to Theseus, appreciate the help from Ariadne, and endeavor to kill the beast and survive.

Similarly, Shakespeare used the locations of the Forest and the Labyrinth to create a muddle of Chaos where his characters could unravel themselves. Many of his plays provide for the characters leaving, returning, testing, retrying, attempting, going up and down stairs, through doorways, and behind curtains, and coming in and coming out. He cleverly used physical movement

---

74. Baring and Cashford, *The Myth of the Goddess*, 140.

from within to without, from one wall to the opposite wall, along trails that dead-end to halls, and through corridors that provide escape in many of his works. His Chaos symbolism in *A Midsummer Night's Dream* closely mirrors what was found in busy London at the end of the sixteenth century, namely congestion, noise, shouting, narrow streets, vagrants and criminals, shoppers and hawkers, immigrants, and workers. Because Shakespeare's audience at the Globe Theatre was an urban one (or at least its members were in South-wark, London, when they watched the play), they were both escaping their crowded life by enjoying *A Midsummer Night's Dream* and at the same time experiencing their life's chaos all over again, simply in an imaginary setting. At least they could relate to it. It is this type of literary celebration of Chaos that most epitomizes the Labyrinth.

The Labyrinth: Modern Mazes in Cityscape and Film

As mentioned in chapter 2, the 2014 dystopian film *The Maze Runner* is a gold mine of Abyss imagery. It features a dynamic, literal labyrinth with high walls, posts, pillars, and monsters—terrifying beasts called Grievers that are machinistic and deadly. The characters journey back and forth between the Valley, the Void-like empty meadow where they live, and the Maze, the Chaos-like labyrinth filled with tall walls, posts, twists, turns, narrow paths, and dead ends. Some of the characters survey the Maze over a long period of time, and one maps out its boundaries and features, even crafting a model of it to help others navigate its passageways. This is the first step in creating Order out of Chaos.

Equally as harrowing, the Triwizard Maze in *Harry Potter and the Goblet of Fire* features green hedges as the walls of a labyrinth. While the book by J. K. Rowling describes monsters and other creatures attacking the tournament champions inside the maze, the film adaptation shows the entangled hedges coming alive themselves as threats, literally reaching out and pulling the heroes into their leaves and vines. This is an instance of the Labyrinth not only portraying a form or location of the World Journey but also becoming the Beast itself, similar to Alister Grierson's portrayal of the Cavern in the film *Sanctum*. Hidden deep within the Triwizard Maze is a portkey, a magical object that physically transports the people to another place and dimension, making quick work of the ultimate quest to find answers and move forward.

But author J. K. Rowling used labyrinthine imagery in far more innovative ways than simply the Triwizard Maze. Her books are overflowing with maze and labyrinth images including the twisting, turning staircases that shift a traveler's destination; portkeys that move one through time and space; portals and cabinets and Rooms of Requirement that transport a person through physical and time-bound barriers. Hogwarts castle consists of hidden doors, secret passageways, and tubes and pipes that twist and tangle within the walls. Rowling's characters pop in and out of the maze of campus from the terrifying forest to Hagrid's cabin to a rookery to study halls, seldom in the same location within an hour and often rebounding on their path because of a discovery or a setback. These are all images of the Labyrinth, the fifth location in which heroes and heroines navigate their journeys of self-growth.

Even theme parks around the world have created popular mazes—many based on *Alice's Adventures in Wonderland*. Parks in Shanghai and Paris have recreated the complex steps taken by the young heroine on her journey to self-discovery, imitating the twists and turns (and growths and shrinkages) experienced by Alice before she returned to reality. And other parks have spun on the idea of the yellow brick road in *The Wonderful Wizard of Oz*, crafting actual pathways upon which parkgoers can walk to recreate a journey of fantasy. These real places where adults and children can go to experience the adventure of a labyrinth are both fun and harrowing, comical and frightening. They bring to life the character's story in a way that lets people act it out in a safe way, though commercialism may dampen much of the symbolic teachings.

In Tolkein's *Lord of the Rings: The Fellowship of the Ring*, the hobbits and their company travel through the deadly Mines of Moria, a dark, cavernous labyrinth of tunnels, mines, wells, passageways, stairs, pits, and dead ends. It is a multilevel chasm with mountains and valleys within mountains and valleys, and the members of the group find themselves retracing their steps, guessing directions, circling back, and at times wandering aimlessly. Here, the concept of a labyrinth is as much about its antiquity as it is about confusion; the mines are ancient and the beasts that inhabit it are so old their identities have been lost. The characters discover lost remnants of the past and even the desiccated corpses of ancestors who died long before. The disconcerting element of twisting, forgotten *time* is as much a challenge of the Labyrinth as is the physical maze of structures.

Even cities and cityscapes can appear as Labyrinths in story and film, with the seeker small on the sidewalk, looking up among towering buildings that dwarf the individual and create obstacles. The labyrinthine idea of an "any-city" metropolis jungle is seen in several of the Marvel Comics and Avengers movies as well as DC Comics films where Superman battles evil in a city named Metropolis and Batman fights crime in Gotham City. These places are nondescript any-cities where the heroes wage ferocious conflicts amid faceless buildings, skyscrapers, bridges, overpasses, sidewalks, statues, intersections, and roadways. This image is particularly poignant because our minds know that there must be thousands if not millions of people living in such a large metropolis, but the nonhuman nature of the cityscape adds to the feeling of Chaos and Void and to the perception of the seeker facing loneliness and isolation.

Finally, several children's films use the technique of "shrinking" a person, forcing the character to navigate through giant and imposing structures that are, in real life, normal. When tiny, the children in the Walt Disney Pictures *Honey, I Shrunk the Kids* face enormous obstacles such as grass and ants, their otherwise boring backyard turning into a gigantic labyrinth-like Abyss. Its hazards include being stepped on, falling into holes, and being eaten by common insects that are mundane in reality, but when writ large, they become massive challenges that mimic the huge obstacles faced in real life. This echoes the theme of small size seen in both *Alice's Adventures in Wonderland* and the 1726 novel by Jonathan Swift, *Gulliver's Travels*. In this swashbuckling tale, Swift relates the adventure of Gulliver, whose boat is blown away at sea by strong winds into strange and distant lands. First, he lands in Lilliput, where people are small, and he is considered a giant. But when he later lands in the land of Brobdingnag, he is the small one—and he faces hazards such as escaping from bees, puppies, and monkeys. Looking outward at a giant land from the perspective of a small person, Gulliver becomes nicer.

Alice: Her Adventure in the Labyrinth

While most of the labyrinths constructed around the world are structures made of bushes or rocks, the symbolism of the labyrinth can also be applied to concepts—to thoughts, mental meanderings, and the confusion of the mind. We all operate in a labyrinth of some kind when we stop and start, fail and try again, lose something or forget something. One of the meanings of a labyrinth was a structure to trap a monster; the conceptual idea is much more immediate and personal and can frustrate us to no end.

I use the word *end* here purposefully because the idea of a labyrinth is that it goes on and on in fits and starts and is such a maze and jumble of directions that there is no easy beginning and no definite end. When we are in a labyrinth, we experience Chaos at its finest; truth feels arbitrary and decisions make no sense. A mental labyrinth is as much a challenge as a physical one, and author Lewis Carroll wasted no time employing this concept in his nonsensical 1865 novel *Alice's Adventures in Wonderland* and its 1871 sequel *Through the Looking-Glass and What Alice Found There.*

These stories brim with Abyss imagery, including accessing alternative realities with portals, transitions, falling into chasms, crossing water, and incredible physical transformations. Alice falls down a deep rabbit hole and enters a new world where she quite literally transforms by changing size. Later, a baby transforms into a pig, and in the sequel, Alice doesn't fall through a rabbit hole but steps into a mirror-portal, arriving, again, in a new land. There, to gain access to each new "realm" in the checkerboard, Alice must cross various brooks of rushing water; at one point she crosses a brook, and her companion transforms into an animal. Upon crossing the last (seventh) brook, Alice is immediately transformed into a queen and crowned. Carroll packed these stories with imagery of transformation, using the World Journey locations of the Cavern, the Deep, and the Forest in both novels.

Alice's Adventures in Wonderland is ripe with labyrinth imagery, and we'll explore just a small bit of it in this short adaptation of a section from the book to grasp just how maddening the path of a (real or figurative) labyrinth can be. Let's listen in on Alice's bizarre and convoluted conversation with the Caterpillar.

— A Story: Alice and the Caterpillar —

Alice had already descended and shrunk and grown again and shrunk again. She was feeling bewildered and unsure she was really Alice anymore. Escaping a group of animals who wanted to oust her, she ran into the forest and came upon a mushroom. Atop the mushroom sat a Caterpillar smoking a hookah.

"Who are you?" asked the Caterpillar.

"I hardly know, sir, just at present," replied Alice. "At least I know who I was when I got up this morning, but I think I must have been changed several times since then."

"Explain yourself," said the Caterpillar.

"I can't explain myself, I'm afraid, sir," said Alice, "because I'm not myself, you see."

"I don't see."

"Being so many different sizes in a day is very confusing."

"It isn't," replied the Caterpillar.

"Well, perhaps your feelings may be different," said Alice. "All I know is, it would feel very strange to me."

"You! Who are you?"

Alice was growing weary of this back-and-forth. "I can't remember things like I used to," she told him. "My size changes every ten minutes!"

He suggested she recite a familiar poem, which she did and botched all the wording and phrases.

"That is not said right," said the Caterpillar.

"Not quite right, I'm afraid," said Alice. "Some of the words have got altered."

"It is wrong from beginning to end." The Caterpillar paused. "What size do you want to be?"

"I'm not particular to size," Alice answered. "Only one doesn't like changing so often, you know."

"I don't know."

Alice said nothing. She had never been so much contradicted in all her life.

Finally, the Caterpillar directed her to eat one side of the mushroom to grow taller and the other to grow shorter. But when Alice nibbled a bit, she immediately shrank so quickly that her chin was pressed closely against her foot. She nibbled another bit and found herself elongated so much that her neck stretched far beneath her eyes. She was "delighted to find that her neck would bend about easily in any direction, like a serpent. She had just succeeded in curving it down into a graceful zigzag" when a bird flew into her face.[75]

———

The story continues with mad, twisting adventures that test Alice in shape, form, age, and temperament. She continues to meet bizarre characters and shift and transform until she awakens from her nap on the banks of the river, where she started, and recalls her "curious dream."

The Labyrinth: Space and Time

Having explored a variety of locations and extremes on the World Journey, including the Cavern and the Deep, you may be wondering about space and time. These concepts are popular in modern film as a location of a character's quest, whether the seeker is traveling to space in a spaceship or bending time using any number of technological machines. Yet traveling into space is not necessarily descent, is it? It's going outward, or so it seems. While researching this book, I came to believe it represents the Labyrinth quite well. Even though the characters in the story are going out to space, they are entering a confusing and convoluted labyrinthian maze built with portals, planets, and black holes.

The notion of time as a labyrinth is explored in *Star Wars*, and it's no accident that the film includes many familiar World Journey themes. Director George Lucas modeled his plot directly on Joseph Campbell's Hero's Journey, and later the philosopher and the filmmaker met face-to-face and developed a lasting friendship. The *Star Wars* films vividly incorporate all the elements of the stages of self-discovery outlined in Campbell's book *The Hero with a*

———

75. Carroll, *Alice's Adventures in Wonderland*, 33.

Thousand Faces, especially the idea of circling from one end of the maze to another through a portal, an idea central to many space films.[76] The concept of traveling from one location to another not through ordinary physical means but by bending forces of nature is a mesmerizing idea, and it's celebrated by the many colorful portals throughout science fiction. It is this nonlinear aspect of the quest that makes time and space travel such a demonstration of the Labyrinth, where the seeker carries the answers to questions that could have helped them avoid the thorny questions in the first place.

This labyrinthine notion of interdimensionality is especially present in the 2014 film *Interstellar*, directed by Christopher Nolan. The lead character played by Matthew McConaughey even describes the time-bending concept of space travel by drawing two points on a piece of paper and bending the paper so the points meet—a nice description of flexible time as a force within the Abyss and a sneaky way of describing the Labyrinth. Throughout the film, characters are seeing hints or shadows of others who have been lost to time but are in fact very close in physical dimension, like being on the other side of a tall wall in a labyrinthine maze. In *Interstellar* as well as *Star Wars*, the characters battle beasts throughout the time dimensions and the physical mazes of outer space, and they accept support from the Guides who help them Resurrect/return.

The circuitous routes taken by Marty McFly and Dr. Emmett Brown in Robert Zemeckis's 1985 hit *Back to the Future* are a fun reference to time as the Labyrinth. Back and forth, the characters reach one point, return, go off to another point, and return again and again, a never-still movement, which is a hallmark of both mazes and time travel. Even goofy movies such as *Bill & Ted's Excellent Adventure* poke fun at the idea, but they still include key components of the quest, such as having a Guide (in *Bill & Ted's*, the guide is none other than George Carlin). And of course, one of the earliest written works regarding possible time travel was H. G. Wells's late nineteenth-century dystopian novella *The Time Machine*. In it, his character travels hundreds of thousands of years into the future, and it is not so much a Labyrinth as a one-way street, yet it sets the stage for new thoughts on the idea of time bending, circuitous routes, and a nonlinear path of discovery.

---

76. Seastrom, "Mythic Discovery Within the Inner Reaches of Outer Space."

These pop-culture examples approach the idea of the Labyrinth in different ways. In *Back to the Future*, the hero learns about himself (and also his parents) and saves the world. In *Bill & Ted's Excellent Adventure*, the heroes exploit the ability to time travel to have a good time and get some schoolwork done. But in *The Time Machine*, the end is odd, and there is no positive epiphany. Instead, the traveler has gone so far into the future that all he finds are ruins, a new species of human that he cannot communicate with, and a sense of despair. He travels even further into the future—thirty million years—to find Earth's civilization collapsed. This grim journey is not about growth and transformation; a true Labyrinth story finds the hero overcoming challenges and making some sort of progress regarding maturity, skill, or human capacity.

Spider Grandmother: Following the Thread

One thing that separates the Labyrinth from the other locations of the World Journey is that it is not static. In other words, it's based on movement, whereas the Cavern, the Deep, and the Vessel are all single entities wherein the hero goes to learn. (The Forest could also be seen as a single entity, although the seeker must travel through it, much like the Labyrinth.) In the Labyrinth, the hero is walking, dancing, or otherwise moving from one location to another and then another, constantly twisting and turning on their quest. This image recalls the weaving of threads on a loom, where threads go one way and then another, creating a tapestry. The image of weaving is inherent in the idea of a labyrinth, in which one starts and stops, returns and doubles back, like the warp and weft, and as we saw in the popular Labyrinth story of Theseus and the Minotaur, the real hero was Ariadne, who provided Theseus with a ball of thread so he could find his way back out. The thread is important because the hero or heroine moves throughout the journey and must then navigate his or her way back.

In his quirky book *Follow This Thread*, author Henry Eliot calls attention to Shakespeare's use of thread in his play *A Midsummer Night's Dream*, likely written between 1594 and 1596.[77] The play is awash in twisty labyrinthine imagery, and Shakespeare makes no pretense of being symbolic or secretive.

---

77. Shakespeare, *A Midsummer Night's Dream*.

Instead, his convoluted play includes references to mazes, threads, and the ancient Greek story of the Minotaur and its heroes Theseus and Ariadne. The play's characters include Duke Theseus; a weaver of thread named Nick Bottom, whom the trickster Puck curses with the head of a donkey; and a group of hormone-saturated teenagers lost on the meandering trails of a deep forest. It also includes impersonated voices and magic juices that impede vision, and as Eliot tells his readers, the name *Bottom* refers to the spindle at the center of a used ball of thread.[78]

In a similar way, the Native American story of Spider Grandmother is a lovely example of a labyrinth and thread story. Told by the Kiowa people of the Great Plains in the central United States, the story involves not only the silken threads from the body of wise Spider Grandmother but also the cupping of the sun in a small vessel to share for light within a dark world. Another tale from the Muscogee (Creek) of Oklahoma reads more as a creation myth where animals earn their black fur, singed tails, or burned heads by trying to carry the sun. A similar tale also appears in Cherokee storytelling, while the following adaptation shares a bit more about the quest of Spider Grandmother and is adapted from the stories of the Kiowa and Muscogee peoples.

——— A STORY: SPIDER GRANDMOTHER ———

At first, the world was dark. There was nothing but darkness, and the animals stubbed their toes when they walked—their hoofed toes and their furry toes. The birds were afraid to fly in the dark. The Animal Council met to decide what to do about it, but nothing worked. The Rabbit tried to fix the darkness but couldn't. The Fox tried but couldn't. The Eagle and Woodpecker both tried. The world stayed dark.

Then an old, small voice sounded in the darkness. It was Spider Grandmother. "I will seek a solution," she said. The other animals laughed at her, as she was just a tiny spider. If the mighty Rabbit and Fox and Eagle and Woodpecker could not fix the dark, how could she? But Spider Grandmother set out on her long journey to find light,

---

78. Eliot, *Follow This Thread.*

slipping her silk out behind her as she went. She crisscrossed rivers, went left and right, crossed deserts and mountains and lakes. At one point, she pulled up a handful of soft clay and fashioned it into a small bowl, which she carried with her. At long last, Spider Grandmother saw an orange light on the horizon and knew she was approaching the Sun People.

Finally, she rested and hid herself out of sight of the Sun People. When the time was right, she reached out and snipped off a small bit of the great orange fire that lit the sky, and she tucked it into her bowl. Then she turned, picked up her thread, and began following the silk to return home.

As she walked home, the fire in her bowl grew larger and larger, brighter and brighter, warmer and warmer until finally she threw it up into the air. It stayed there and became the sun, lighting the world with a beautiful glow. But wise Spider Grandmother kept a tiny piece of the sun in her bowl, and she shared it with her people so they could build their fires, bake their clay, and cook their food.

———

Other tales share that Spider Grandmother connected a bit of her silken web to every living being upon birth so she could find them throughout their lives. This sort of weaving of birth and direction, life and purpose, is at the core of the long and twisting voyage that embodies the Labyrinth.

In the end, it's what the ancient labyrinth originated as: a dance through space, a meandering of questions and answers, paths, and turns. Essentially, the Labyrinth and its thread form a way to get back to ourselves. The underlying theme of never-ending self-discovery has made the Labyrinth an enduring classic of human consciousness and an essential location in World Journey stories.

EPILOGUE

Failure and Success on the World Journey

Until now, we've looked at stories where the seeker faces a challenge and succeeds, emerging from their quest more resilient, more mature, and stronger than before. These are the influential, symbolic stories that have survived for generations.

But what about when the hero fails? Are there stories that illustrate what happens when a person doesn't go into the dark or doesn't get eaten by the Beast or doesn't follow the Guide or—ultimately—fails to change? In fact, there are very few. Of all the stories I came across in researching the World Journey, all portrayed success after adversity—except three, and interestingly, the first two owe their genesis to the story of Jonah and the Whale.

When the Hero Fails

None of us want to fail in our own personal journeys. Yet this is exactly what happens in two works of relatively modern fiction. Each displays the discouragement and suffering that occurs when the potential inherent in facing a challenge is overlooked by the character. These are Herman Melville's novel *Moby Dick* and J. M. Barrie's character Captain Hook.

Jonah's descent and battle with the whale was an inspiration for *Moby Dick*. But whereas Jonah was consumed by the beast and emerged reborn with a higher consciousness, Captain Ahab, the main character of the story, fails. Ahab is obsessed with the great whale Moby Dick, and he sails across the ocean to hunt the beast and kill it. Captain Ahab parallels Marduk fighting the sea serpent Tiamat, the great beast of the deep, and he shares much in common with the biblical Jonah facing his whale. Yet the story of Ahab ends very differently. He does not emerge victorious. Instead, his fanatical sense of vengeance causes him to fail in his efforts, and the whale wins, dragging him down into the salty deep. Ahab never discovers his potential and he never realizes immortal consciousness from the Serpent, the Beast. Instead, he fails to make the necessary sacrifices (forgiveness, collaboration, etc.), and he fails to emerge from the Abyss. Instead, he dies.

In this instance, the potential hero completes the journey downward, descending into a watery realm where he has the opportunity to contemplate, to ponder, and to emerge transformed as a man without vengeance who is capable of forgiveness. But Ahab can't. This is one of the few stories that shows the consequences of *failure* in the Abyss instead of success. Instead of the Deep and the Serpent representing agents of enlightenment, they are vehicles of death, and the death is due to the hero's inability to transform from a man of hatred to a man of forgiveness and humility. When given the opportunity to discover his true Self and make changes that would help him emerge into a new life, Ahab squanders his chance and loses his life.

Melville's story later inspired J. M. Barrie to create the character Captain Hook in his popular children's book *Peter Pan*, published in 1911. Hook loses a duel to Peter Pan, who kicks him overboard into the salty sea (*potential*) and into the open maw not of a whale but of another type of sea serpent—a crocodile (*immortality*). The beast consumes his hand, and Hook thereafter obsessively seeks revenge against it. Like Ahab, Hook loses, and he is eventually swallowed whole by the crocodile and dies—an instance of being consumed by the Beast but without being released, resulting not in epiphany but in death.

Owen and the Slumber King

Those previous two tragic stories are among the rare few that point directly to the dire consequences of failing to achieve personal growth. The third is a Welsh folktale called "The Slumber King." It features many images we are familiar with, including the hazel tree of wisdom, a hidden passageway that leads down into a deep cavern, and a foe that is ready to kill the hero. In this tale, a young lad named Owen is shown the way to retrieve riches hidden in the earth, and he is also taught how to leave safely. He should be able to provide for his family for the rest of his life, but instead of emerging victorious and wise, Owen displays greed and carelessness, and he is murdered in the cavern.

— A STORY: OWEN AND THE SLUMBER KING —

The young lad Owen had left his homeland of Wales, taking his hazel walking stick, and was standing on the London Bridge, looking out over the city, when he heard his name called.

"Owen!" said the voice. The boy turned to see a stranger looking at him. "Tell me," said the man, "where did you get that walking stick?"

"Growing in a forest in Wales," Owen replied.

The man told him that under the hazel tree where he harvested his stick was a cavern filled with gold. "Take me there," the man said, and the boy agreed and led the man from London all the way to Wales. They crossed mountains and valleys and rivers and finally emerged at a great old hazel tree. "Help me dig!" said the man, and they proceeded to dig up the bush. In the ground underneath, Owen saw a large disk of stone, and when he unearthed it, he saw a passageway and stairs leading down into the darkness. The man lit a torch and led Owen deep into the earth.

In the middle of the passageway was a silver bell hanging from the ceiling. "Don't touch it!" warned the man. "It will wake them up." They traveled further down the passageway until they arrived at a great open cavern. The boy gasped; there were countless soldiers sleeping in the dark, surrounded by heaps of gold and silver. "Take the gold or the silver," whispered the man to Owen, "and you'll be rich." Owen began to fill his pockets and clothing with as much gold as he could carry, and he turned to go back up the passageway. But the man warned him again: "Don't touch the bell! If you do, the men will wake. If they do, be sure to call out, 'Not now!' and they'll return to their slumber."

Owen struggled under the weight of his heavy load up the passageway and managed to squeeze by the bell without waking anyone. He went to his parents and bought them everything they wanted, and more for himself. He wasted years spending his money on gambling and extravagance until one day he found himself impoverished. He decided to return to the cavern.

He went to the base of the hazel tree, lifted the disk of stone, and descended the passageway, avoiding the bell. Once again, he filled his pockets and clothing with gold, but on his trip up the passage, he bumped into the bell. Instantly the warriors awoke, but careless Owen had forgotten what to call out. Within seconds, the men attacked him until he bled, and they threw him out of the passageway. He crawled to his village where he lived crippled and poor the remainder of his days.

———

As a quest-turned-morality tale, this story teaches children what will happen if they are greedy, careless, or simpleminded. It's a reminder of how being shallow and selfish will ruin a life, even if the story is cloaked in whisperings of King Arthur.

When the Hero Succeeds

It seems fair to say that failure is not the point of World Journey stories. These stories exist to teach us to travel the path from Abyss to epiphany successfully. All the other heroes we've discussed have struck out on the Journey, suffered the tests, and emerged changed: Gilgamesh returns with the plant; Inanna climbs the stairs to become the goddess of the seasons; Persephone emerges from the Cavern not as a young girl but as womanly queen of the Underworld; Beowulf completes his tasks and emerges as a hero having saved his countrymen from danger; Odysseus and Aeneas emerge from the Underworld with greater knowledge and understanding about what awaits them in the afterlife; Madchen emerges from her time with Frau Holle, or Mother Winter, as a courageous (and richer) young woman; Misiti develops her inner courage when she plucks the lion's whisker; Jonah is released from the whale and emerges from the Deep not as a coward but as a responsible missionary; Semele is released from the chest as a newborn; Gwion changes from a kitchen boy to the great poet Merlin; Snow White, Rapunzel, Beauty, and Vasalisa grow from innocent children to capable adult women; and Theseus emerges as a (questionable) hero from the Labyrinth.

Change is critical, and a healthy acceptance of the natural changes in one's life will lead to satisfaction and a sense of fulfillment. But these stories of the World Journey also teach us that success is not necessarily what we thought it was going to be when we entered. Persephone, for instance, achieves maturity and becomes a great queen, but instead of living above land with her mother for the rest of her life, she must spend part of her year in the Underworld. Gilgamesh finds the plant of immortality, but his true success is in losing that plant to the snake, a symbolic agent of change, achieving understanding and awareness but not the immortality he was searching for. Eve's idea of success may have been to gain understanding from the Tree of the Knowledge of Good and Evil, but it thrust her into the world of reality and form, allowing her to pursue a fulfilling life as a mortal and mother but not in the garden as she had expected.

Our Responsibilities as Readers and Writers

We all experience the telling of stories throughout our lives, whether we're watching TV, reading books, or listening to tales around a campfire. Storytelling is part of our humanity and an enjoyable way we connect with others, and storycraft is a valuable skill and contribution to civilization. Yet, it's important to remember that when we are listening to, reading, or watching a story, it is up to us to do several things:

- We must recognize when symbols or metaphors are being used. Often, a story is so engrossing we become emotionally tied to the plot or the characters, and we forget that some of it is symbolic. Symbolism both distorts reality (think of the meaning of colors) and teaches lessons (think of courage on a quest). As viewers and readers, we must watch for these symbols and be aware of their use in a story.

- We must recognize that symbols or metaphors can be fallible, especially when tying meaning to a culture, ethnic group, gender, or way of life. Cultural appropriation was common in stories of the past and still makes up characters or plotlines in books and films today. It's up to us to notice these and call them out, teaching children and others that symbols are powerful devices that can either help or hurt. Using imagery to support and build a person's confidence is to be commended; using it to destroy or tarnish a person or community based on color, size, voice, or other element should be avoided.

- We must also share stories widely and help others, especially children, analyze and deconstruct what they're reading so they can think proactively and appreciate the creative spirit of storycraft. We must share stories from other cultures so others can see the differences and similarities (isn't it fascinating how the Serpent is used in so many ways?).

- It's important for us to look for the five locations of the World Journey and explore how each location influences the characters or the plot. This is not so much so you can pick apart a story but so you can feel connected to the thousands of stories from around the globe that teach lessons through someone's adventures in the Cavern, the Deep, the Vessel, the Forest, or the Labyrinth.

- There are also responsibilities for writers and film directors. Some readers here may be screenwriters, editors, directors, assistants, or college instructors sharing details about the world of film. Just as we have responsibilities as readers and viewers, we can improve and strengthen the world by integrating symbols and metaphors positively throughout the creation of new works. Leverage your understanding of imagery to create new meanings, share innovative concepts, and use the concepts and locations of the World Journey to bring light and understanding to cultures and communities seeking inclusion and peace.

Your Personal World Journey

In most of these myths and tales, success happens and failure is averted. The stories can sometimes seem like distant allegories meant for someone else. We may understand, academically, that Descent and Resurrection come at a cost, but what exactly does that look like in the real world? How do you see this in your own life?

This is where application of the imagery comes into play. We are the lead characters in our own lives, and we're facing challenges just as poignant and scary as those faced by any character in the stories. Our challenges are real, yet our entire point in living is to face them and achieve our own levels of success. These levels look different for each of us and at various times of our lives, but they are united in theme: puberty, passion, purpose; a wider understanding; a deeper calling; answers to our questions; growth, creativity, epiphany.

We must ask ourselves each time, with each challenge we face, especially the scary, mighty, daunting challenges that shake us: Is it worth it? Am I worth it? Can I do it? Reading the tales of our ancient ancestors can help us recognize symbolism, but only by asking yourself the important questions will you truly get to the right answers. The right answer will open a door that you might not have considered, and it will point you down a path you might not have taken. Then you'll face another challenge and another question. Like the colorful locations of the World Journey, your answers will shape and influence the rest of your story.

The following section is titled "Book Group Resource," but everyone is welcome to explore it, whether you're in a book group or not. It offers questions to help you deepen your understanding of the imagery and metaphors presented in this book and to dive wholeheartedly into exploring your own sense of challenge, adventure, and life purpose. Sit with a friend over tea or coffee, ask each other these questions, and take your time to find and discuss the answers. Sometimes you'll think of something that happened to you just yesterday, while other answers may emerge from the webs spun across the time and space of your life. Use these questions as a chance to ponder, to realize, and also to celebrate the wonderful story that is life.

Our understanding of fairy tale, myth, and film is enriched by the symbolic locations in which the stories take place, turning quest literature into lessons of life and love. Understanding these five places on the World Journey that have been central to stories of Descent and Resurrection since time immemorial—the Cavern, the Deep, the Vessel, the Forest, and the Labyrinth—is key to appreciating the great works of symbolic storytelling...and to enjoying the fantastic adventures told across four thousand years of our collective human experience.

Book Group Resource

The point of all the colorful, sweeping, epic, and enchanting imagery in myth, text, and tale is to relate the process of change and to transcend one stage of life and enter another—preferably a better one but most certainly a more mature one. We shift from birth to infancy to childhood to adolescence to adulthood to death. Each of these stages requires the individual to change physically, emotionally, socially, mentally, and spiritually into a form of the Self that is stronger and more resilient, kinder, wiser, or happier.

This resource is meant to support exploration and deeper understanding for those reading and learning in a community, especially in book groups. Please use the following questions to stimulate reflection and discussion about personal growth, life's purpose, societal change and beliefs, and the fascinating origins of creativity.

Recognizing Imagery of the Journey in Your Own Life

People enter the World Journey for many reasons. Complacency and boredom are triggers. Children may be ready to sexually mature, and adults might need a more open perspective of the world. Understanding the patterns of life and death with a greater spiritual sensitivity can require us to overcome surprisingly tough challenges. Some people enter the Abyss involuntarily—they are thrust into it due to difficult life circumstances beyond their control. Other people embark on the process of fulfillment and change for any number of reasons, and regardless of the reason, the goal is always the same: to emerge from this terrifying and transformative place—and process—a better person.

It's not an easy place or a simple process; the World Journey will test you. It takes gritty work to enact a change so substantial that you "birth" a vital part of yourself that was previously hidden or ignored. Epiphany is like a baby chick breaking through its eggshell; what was formerly a smooth, perfect shell is suddenly cracked and utterly destroyed. But what emerges is new life.

Tragedies can happen over which we have little control, but we can shape what comes next constructively. We can also use this imagery voluntarily when we are at that jumping-off point—ready for a change and knowing that something in our lives must shift so that a breakthrough can happen.

Imagery can help us do that. These stories are not a program nor a template nor a policy nor a religion. Symbolic stories can provide that "aha!" moment when you see in someone else's suffering and courage that you, too, have the ability to turn circumstances into something positive. These myths and folktales show us how others have done it, and though most are fiction, they are written from a collective understanding of a person's artistic or creative process and the universal stages of physical, emotional, and spiritual growth. The symbols of enlightenment are tools, and you can put them in your toolbox to help you as an individual, as an artist, and as a social being in relationships of every stripe. Upon the lip of the Vessel of the Deep, we can dive into—or sail across to—epiphany.

Book Group Questions

It can be extremely helpful to explore these ideas and concepts within the safety of a welcoming group, such as a book club. I encourage you to think about the metaphors and imagery in terms of the social context or life outside yourself, including historic and contemporary events, as well as your personal experiences. Each of us has lived through (and will continue to live through) events and experiences that will challenge and shape us. Looking at these experiences using the images and locations explored in this book can support a vibrant examination of what got you where you are and how you may best move forward.

———

Use the following questions to guide your discussion:

1. Do you think of your life as an adventure? Why or why not?

2. Where in your life have you experienced Descent? What hardships did you encounter?

3. Have you been supported by a Guide? What role does mentorship play in your life?

4. Can you recall a time when you thought a Guide was a true mentor but instead he or she was a false guide? What did you learn from this experience?

5. Have you been a Guide for someone else? How did you support or encourage this person on their path?

6. What might Resurrection look like for you—personally or professionally? What if it looks different from what you expect (or hope)?

7. What are other examples of Abyss imagery in modern tales and film?

8. How does crossing water make you feel? Do you find that your spirit is renewed when you sail or spend time around water?

9. How does music or dance enhance our experience of tales of the World Journey? How do you nurture the "creative urge"?

10. Is it misogynistic to think of passive potential as feminine and active formation as masculine? Why is it necessary to have both for creation—and for the creative impulse?

11. What is epiphany? Is it elusory and transient, or can it last?

12. Can adults understand the same inherent messages in fairy tales that children can? And with what impact or result?

13. In what ways are Chaos and the Void the same? Which one speaks to you more and is more helpful or transformative in your life?

14. Does the dreamworld serve a purpose for you? Is it a place of respite or work?

15. How does the labyrinth that we sometimes walk (made of stones or plants) resemble the symbolic Labyrinth of stories? How does it support the inner consciousness in bending time or space?

16. What would a thread look like for you? How could someone offer support that would "guide you back to yourself"?

17. How is time a labyrinth? What's the difference between a circle and a spiral—especially in terms of time? Can we use the World Journey to enhance our experience of time and get the most out of every day?

18. As you take twists and turns, make decisions, and follow your own Labyrinth throughout your life, do you find that you leave a trail of thread behind you? Is this a skill that you've learned? Does it help to have a thread that can get you back on track if you get lost? In what way does the thread appear in your life? As a friend? A family member? A mentor or teacher? A philosophy that you live by?

Films and Books Referenced

2001: A Space Odyssey (Stanley Kubrick, dir., 1968)

The Abyss (James Cameron, dir., 1989)

Alice's Adventures in Wonderland (Lewis Carroll, 1865)

Back to the Future (Robert Zemeckis, dir., 1985)

Batman Begins (Christopher Nolan, dir., 2005)

Beauty and the Beast (Gabrielle-Suzanne Barbot de Villeneuve, 1740)

Bill & Ted's Excellent Adventure (Stephen Herek, dir., 1989)

The Cave (Bruce Hunt, dir., 2005)

The Fellowship of the Ring (J R. R. Tolkien, 1954)

Follow This Thread: A Maze Book to Get Lost In (Henry Eliot, 2019)

The Goonies (Richard Donner, dir., 1985)

Gulliver's Travels (Jonathan Swift, 1726)

Harry Potter and the Deathly Hallows (J. K. Rowling, 2007)

Harry Potter and the Goblet of Fire (J. K. Rowling, 2000)

The Heart of the World: A Journey to the Last Secret Place (Ian Baker, 2004)

The Hobbit (J. R. R. Tolkien, 1937)

Honey, I Shrunk the Kids (Joe Johnston, dir., 1989)

Interstellar (Christopher Nolan, dir., 2014)

It's a Wonderful Life (Frank Capra, dir., 1946)

Journey to the Center of the Earth (Eric Brevig, dir., 2008)

Journey to the Center of the Earth (Jules Verne, 1864)

Jurassic Park (Michael Crichton, 1990)

Jurassic Park (Steven Spielberg, dir., 1993)

Life of Pi (Ang Lee, dir., 2012)

Life of Pi (Yann Martel, 2001)

The Lion, the Witch and the Wardrobe (C. S. Lewis, 1950)

The Little Mermaid (Hans Christian Andersen, 1837)

The Little Mermaid (John Musker and Ron Clements, dirs., 1989)

Lord of the Rings: The Fellowship of the Ring (J. R. R. Tolkien, 1954)

The Maze Runner (James Dashner, 2009)

The Maze Runner (Wes Ball, dir., 2014)

A Midsummer Night's Dream (William Shakespeare, 1595)

Moby Dick; Or, The Whale (Herman Melville, 1851)

O Brother, Where Art Thou? (Joel Coen and Ethan Coen, dirs.; 2000)

Optimism, an Essay (Helen Keller, 1903)

Peter Pan (James Matthew Barrie, 1911)

Pinocchio (Ben Sharpsteen and Hamiliton Luske, dirs., 1940)

The Polar Express (Robert Zemeckis, dir., 2004)

Round the World in 80 Days (Jules Verne, 1872)

Sanctum (Alister Grierson, dir., 2011)

Star Wars: Episode IV – A New Hope (George Lucas, dir., 1977)

Strega Nona (Tomie dePaola, 1975)

Through the Looking-Glass and What Alice Found There (Lewis Carroll, 1871)

The Time Machine (H. G. Wells, 1895)

Twenty Thousand Leagues Under the Sea (Jules Verne, 1870)

What Dreams May Come (Vincent Ward, dir., 1998)

The Wizard of Oz (Victor Fleming, dir., 1939)

The Wonderful Wizard of Oz (L. Frank Baum, 1900)

Bibliography

"A Brief History of Ceramics and Glass." The American Ceramic Society. Accessed February 7, 2024. https://ceramics.org/about/what-are -engineered-ceramics-and-glass/brief-history-of-ceramics-and-glass/.

Aldington, Richard, and Delano Ames, trans. *The New Larousse Encyclopedia of Mythology.* Paris: Prometheus Press, 1968.

Andersen, Hans Christian. "The Little Mermaid" In *Fairy Tales Told for Children.* Copenhagen: C. A. Reitzel, 1836.

Baker, Ian. *The Heart of the World: A Journey to the Last Secret Place.* New York: The Penguin Press, 2004.

Ball, Wes, dir. *The Maze Runner.* Twentieth Century Fox, 2014.

Baring, Anne, and Jules Cashford. *The Myth of the Goddess: Evolution of an Image.* New York: Arkana, 1991.

Barrie, J. M. *Peter Pan.* Originally published as *Peter and Wendy.* London, England: Hodder & Stoughton, 1911. Project Gutenberg, 2021. https://www.gutenberg.org/cache/epub/16/pg16-images.html.

Baum, L. Frank. *The Wonderful Wizard of Oz*. The original 1900 edition. New York: Dover Publications, 1960.

Bettelheim, Bruno. *The Uses of Enchantment: The Meaning and Importance of Fairy Tales*. New York: Vintage Books, 1989.

The Bible: Revised Standard Version Old Testament, RSV New Testament. New York: American Bible Society, 1980.

Blair, Elizabeth. "Why Are Old Women Often the Face of Evil in Fairy Tales and Folklore?" NPR News. October 28, 2015. https://www.wbur.org/npr/450657717/why-are-old-women-often-the-face-of-evil-in-fairy-tales-and-folklore?ft=nprml&f=450657717.

Brevig, Eric, dir. *Journey to the Center of the Earth*. New Line Cinema, 2008.

The Brothers Grimm. *Grimm's Complete Fairy Tales*. Illustrated by Arthur Rackham. New York: Fall River Press, 2014.

———. *Grimm's Fairy Tales*. Illustrated by Arnold Roth. New York: Macmillan, 1963.

Caduto, Michael, and Joseph Bruchac. *Keepers of the Earth: American Stories and Environmental Activities for Children*. Golden, CO: Fulcrum Publishing, 1997.

Cameron, James, dir. *The Abyss*. Twentieth Century Fox, 1989.

Campbell, Joseph. *The Hero with a Thousand Faces*. New York: Pantheon Books, 1949.

———. *The Inner Reaches of Outer Space: Metaphor as Myth and as Religion*. Novato, CA: New World Library, 2002.

———. *Oriental Mythology*. Vol. 2, *The Masks of God*. New York: The Viking Press, 1962.

———. *Pathways to Bliss: Mythology and Personal Transformation*. Edited by David Kudler. Novato, CA: New World Library, 2004.

———. *The Power of Myth*. Edited by Betty Sue Flowers. New York: Doubleday, 1988.

———. *Primitive Mythology*. Vol. 1, *The Masks of God*. New York: The Penguin Group, 1987.

Capra, Frank, dir. *It's a Wonderful Life*. RKO Pictures, 1946.

Carroll, Lewis. *Alice's Adventures in Wonderland.* Mineola, NY: Dover Publications, 1993.

———. *Alice's Adventures in Wonderland; Through the Looking Glass; What Alice Found There; The Hunting of the Snark.* New York: Shocken Books, 1978.

Coen, Joel, and Ethan Coen, dirs. *O Brother, Where Art Thou?* Touchstone Pictures, 2000.

Crosby, Janice C. *Cauldron of Changes: Feminist Spirituality in Fantastic Fiction.* Jefferson, NC: McFarland, 2000.

Crossley-Holland, Kevin. *Between Worlds: Folktales of Britain & Ireland.* Somerville, MA: Candlewick Press, 1997.

Dalley, Stephanie. *Myths from Mesopotamia: Creation, the Flood, Gilgamesh, and Others.* New York: Oxford University Press, 2000. First published 1989.

Davis, Kenneth C. *Don't Know Much about Mythology: Everything You Need to Know about the Greatest Stories in Human History but Never Learned.* New York: HarperCollins Publishers, 2006.

dePaola, Tomie. *Strega Nona.* Englewood Cliffs, NJ: Prentice-Hall, 1975.

Department of Greek and Roman Art. "Death, Burial, and the Afterlife in Ancient Greece." The Metropolitan Museum of Art. October 2003. http://www.metmuseum.org/toah/hd/dbag/hd_dbag.htm.

DeSpain, Pleasant. *Thirty-Three Multicultural Tales to Tell.* Little Rock, AR: August House, 1993.

DK. *The Mythology Book.* The Big Ideas Series. New York: DK Publishing, 2021.

Domonoske, Camila. "Mirror, Mirror: Does 'Fairest' Mean Most Beautiful or Most White?" NPR: Code Switch. May 18, 2014. https://www.npr.org/sections/codeswitch/2014/05/16/313154674/mirror-mirror-does-fairest-mean-most-beautiful-or-most-white.

Donner, Richard, dir. *The Goonies.* Warner Brothers, 1985.

Eliot, Henry. *Follow This Thread: A Maze Book to Get Lost In.* New York: Three Rivers Press, 2018.

"Ester 1: Mordecai's Dream." Revised Standard Version Catholic Edition. Bible Gateway. Accessed March 14, 2015. https://www.biblegateway .com/passage/?search=Esther+1&version=RSVCE.

"Factory Act." The Editors of Encyclopaedia Britannica. March 7, 2023. https://www.britannica.com/event/Factory-Act-United-Kingdom-1833 /additional-info#history.

Fleming, Victor, dir. *The Wizard of Oz.* Technicolor. Metro-Goldwyn-Mayer, 1939.

Gardner, John, and John Maier, trans. *Gilgamesh.* New York: Vintage Books, 1984.

Gould, Joan. *Spinning Straw into Gold: What Fairy Tales Reveal about the Transformations in a Woman's Life.* New York: Random House, 2005.

Gray, Thomas. "The Descent of Odin: An Ode." Thomas Gray Archive. Accessed February 6, 2024. https://www.thomasgray.org/cgi-bin/display .cgi?text=dooo#poem.

Grierson, Alister, dir. *Sanctum.* Universal Pictures, 2011.

Grimal, Pierre, ed, and Patricia Beardsworth, trans. *Larousse World Mythology.* London: Hamlyn, 1965.

Harper, Robert Francis. *Assyrian and Babylonian Literature.* 1904 edition. New York: D. Appleton, 1900.

Herek, Stephen, dir. *Bill and Ted's Excellent Adventure.* Nelson Entertainment, 1989.

Hunt, Bruce, dir. *The Cave.* Sony Pictures Releasing, 2005.

Ions, Veronica. *The History of Mythology.* Surrey, England: CLB Publishing, 1999.

Johnston, Joe, dir. *Honey, I Shrunk the Kids.* Buena Vista Pictures Distribution, 1989.

Jordan, Michael. *The Green Mantle: An Investigation into Our Lost Knowledge of Plants.* London: Cassell, 2001.

Keller, Helen. *Optimism, an Essay.* New York: T.Y. Crowell, 1903.

Kilmer, Joyce. "Trees." *Poetry* 2, no. 5 (August 1915): 153. https://www .poetryfoundation.org/poetrymagazine/poems/12744/trees.

Knapp, Bettina L. *Women in Myth*. New York: State University of New York Press, 1997.

Kramer, Samuel Noah. "Reflections on the Mesopotamian Flood: The Cuneiform Data New and Old." *Expedition Magazine*, Summer 1967. http://www.penn.museum/sites/expedition/reflections-on-the-mesopotamian-flood/.

Kubrick, Stanley, dir. *2001: A Space Odyssey*. Metro-Goldwyn-Mayer, 1968.

Lawson, Mark. "Cape Fear." *Guardian*. September 27, 2006. https://www.theguardian.com/film/2006/sep/27/classics.

Lee, Ang, dir. *Life of Pi*. Fox 2000 Pictures, 2012.

Lewis, C. S. *The Lion, The Witch, and The Wardrobe*. London: Geoffrey Bles, 1950.

Lucas, George, dir. *Star Wars: Episode IV – A New Hope*. Twentieth Century Fox, 1977.

"Matsya." Encyclopedia Britannica. March 16, 2023. https://www.britannica.com/topic/Matsya-Hinduism.

Mark, Joshua J. "Enuma Elish – The Babylonian Epic of Creation – Full Text." World History Encyclopedia. May 04, 2018. https://www.worldhistory.org/article/225/enuma-elish---the-babylonian-epic-of-creation---fu/.

Meister, Cari. *Beauty and the Beast: 3 Beloved Tales*. Stories around the World. North Mankato, MN: Capstone Press, 2017.

Melville, Herman. *Moby Dick; Or, The Whale*. New York: Harper & Brothers, 1851. https://www.gutenberg.org/ebooks/15.

Monaghan, Patricia. *The New Book of Goddesses and Heroines*. 3rd ed. St. Paul, MN: Llewellyn Publications, 2000.

Nolan, Christopher, dir. *Batman Begins*. Warner Bros. Pictures, 2005.

———. *Interstellar*. Paramount Pictures, 2014.

Osbon, Diane, ed. *Reflections on the Art of Living: A Joseph Campbell Companion*. New York: HarperCollins, 1991.

Pagano, Alessandra, and Matteo Dalena. "Dante's 'Inferno' Is a Journey to Hell and Back." *National Geographic*. October 20, 2022. https://www

.nationalgeographic.com/history/history-magazine/article/dantes-inferno
-is-a-journey-to-hell-and-back.

Perrault, Charles. "Little Red Riding Hood." University of Pittsburgh. Last
modified September 21, 2003. https://sites.pitt.edu/~dash/perrault.html.

—————. *Tales of Passed Times*. London, England: J. M. Dent, 1900. Project
Gutenberg, 2010. https://gutenberg.org/files/33511/33511-h/33511
-h.htm.

Philip, Neil. *The Illustrated Book of Myths: Tales and Legends of the World*.
Illustrated by Nilesh Mistry. New York: DK, 1995.

Philip, Neil, and Nicoletta Simborowski, trans. *The Complete Fairy Tales of
Charles Perrault*. With an introduction and notes on the story by Neil
Philip. New York: Clarion Books, 1993.

Philpot, J. H. *The Sacred Tree in Religion and Myth*. Mineola, NY: Dover
Publications, 2004.

Piquero, Juan. "Odysseus: Return of the King." *National Geographic*, March/
April 2023.

Potter, Beatrix. *The Tale of Jemima Puddle Duck*. London: Frederick Warne,
1908.

Price, Paxton. "Victorian Child Labor and the Conditions They Worked In."
Victorian Children. March 2, 2013. https://victorianchildren
.org/victorian-child-labor/.

Rowling, J. K. *Harry Potter and the Deathly Hallows*. New York: Scholastic
Inc., 2007.

—————. *Harry Potter and the Goblet of Fire*. New York: Scholastic Inc.,
2002.

Saint Joseph Edition of the New American Bible. Totowa, NJ: Catholic Book
Publishing Group, 2010.

Seastrom, Lucas. "Mythic Discovery Within the Inner Reaches of Outer
Space: Joseph Campbell Meets George Lucas - Part 1." Star Wars. October 22, 2015. https://www.starwars.com/news/mythic-discovery-within
-the-inner-reaches-of-outer-space-joseph-campbell-meets-george-lucas
-part-i.

Seigneuret, John-Charles, ed. *Dictionary of Literary Themes and Motifs*. New York: Greenwood Press, 1988.

Shakespeare, William. *A Midsummer Night's Dream*. Project Gutenberg. June 26, 2023. https://www.gutenberg.org/files/1514/1514-h/1514-h .htm.

Sharpsteen, Ben, and Hamilton Luske, dirs. *Pinocchio*. RKO Radio Pictures, 1940.

Sjöö, Monica, and Barbara Mor. *The Great Cosmic Mother: Rediscovering the Religion of the Earth*. San Francisco: Harper & Row, 1987.

Spielberg, Steven, dir. *Jurassic Park*. Universal Pictures, 1993.

Starhawk, Diane Baker, and Anne Hill. *Circle Round: Raising Children in Goddess Traditions*. Paperback edition. New York: Bantam Publishers, 1987.

Stone, Merlin. *Ancient Mirrors of Womanhood: A Treasury of Goddess and Heroine Lore from Around the World*. Boston: Beacon Press, 1979.

————. *When God Was a Woman*. New York: Houghton Mifflin Harcourt, 1976.

Strang, Veronica. "Life Down Under: Water and Identity in an Aboriginal Cultural Landscape." *Goldsmiths Anthropology Research Papers*. New Cross, London: University of London, 2002. https://www.gold.ac.uk /media/documents-by-section/departments/anthropology/garp/GARP7 .pdf.

Swift, Jonathan. *Gulliver's Travels*. Project Gutenberg. September 6, 1997. https://www.gutenberg.org/files/829/829-h/829-h.htm.

"Terracotta Bell-Krater (Bowl for Mixing Wine and Water)." The Met. Accessed March 2015. http://www.metmuseum.org/collection/the -collection-online/search/252973.

Thomas, Jacqueline Kay. "Aphrodite Unshamed: James Joyce's Romantic Aesthetics of Feminine Flow." PhD diss., University of Texas, 2007. Microfilm. https://books.google.com/books/about/Aphrodite _Unshamed.html?id=17UDkAEACAAJ.

Tolkien, J. R. R. *The Fellowship of the Ring*. The Lord of the Rings. London: Allen & Unwin, 1954.

Trousdale, Gary, and Kirk Wise, dirs. *Beauty and the Beast*. Walt Disney Pictures, 1991.

Verne, Jules. "Journey to the Center of the Earth." *Education and Entertainment Magazine*. 1867.

Verne, Jules. *Journey to the Center of the Earth; Twenty Thousand Leagues Under the Sea; Round the World in Eighty Days*. With an introduction by Tim Farrant. New York: Alfred A. Knopf, 2013.

Walter, Chip. "First Artists." Photographs by Stephen Alvarez. *National Geographic*, January 2015. http://ngm.nationalgeographic.com/2015 /01/first-artists/alvarez-photography.

Ward, Vincent, dir. *What Dreams May Come*. PolyGram Filmed Entertainment, 1998.

Welles, Marcia L. *Persephone's Girdle: Narratives of Rape in Seventeenth-Century Spanish Literature*. Nashville, TN: Vanderbilt University Press, 2000.

Wells, H. G. *The Time Machine*. New York: New American Library, 2002.

"What Is the Ebers Papyrus?" Leipzig University Library. Accessed February 9, 2024. https://www.ub.uni-leipzig.de/en/about-us/exhibitions /permanent-exhibition/ebers-papyrus/.

Zemeckis, Robert, dir. *Back to the Future*. Universal Pictures, 1985.

——. *The Polar Express*. THQ Inc., 2004.

Zipes, Jack, trans. *The Original Folk and Fairy Tales of the Brothers Grimm: The Complete First Edition*. Princeton: Princeton University Press, 2014.

Index

F

G

H

I

J

K

V

W

Y

© Eli Dagostino

About the Author

Long fascinated by words and imagery, herbalist, author, and international speaker Holly Bellebuono weaves her thirty-year career as an herbalist with curiosity about the human experience. Holly is the author of the award-winning documentary book *Women Healers of the World: The Traditions, History and Geography of Herbal Medicine*, where she interviewed women from cultures around the globe and explored the etymology of words, searching for deeper meaning of the human spirit. Her *Parabola* article "Darkness and the Divine Feminine" and her lecture to the Association for the Study of Women and Myth explore the images of the cavern, darkness, and the mythic abyss, sharing insights from her travels, interviews, and research into people, texts, and narratives. Holly began her research for *Once Upon a Place* because she is a plant-geek and was inspired by the stories of the Descent and Resurrection of the seed. She is eternally charmed by the world's earthy, clever, and mythic tales of transformation and humanity's never-ending quest to learn, grow, and find purpose.

Holly hosts retreats, workshops and courses for individuals and businesses pursuing purpose and entrepreneurship, as well as healing, women's empowerment, and the spirit of growth. She provides business coaching and is the founder of The Bellebuono School of Herbal Medicine. This is Holly's eighth book; learn more at hollybellebuono.com.

To Write to the Author

If you wish to contact the author or would like more information about this book, please write to the author in care of Llewellyn Worldwide Ltd. and we will forward your request. Both the author and the publisher appreciate hearing from you and learning of your enjoyment of this book and how it has helped you. Llewellyn Worldwide Ltd. cannot guarantee that every letter written to the author can be answered, but all will be forwarded. Please write to:

Holly Bellebuono
⁒ Llewellyn Worldwide
2143 Wooddale Drive
Woodbury, MN 55125-2989
Please enclose a self-addressed stamped envelope for reply,
or $1.00 to cover costs. If outside the U.S.A., enclose
an international postal reply coupon.

Many of Llewellyn's authors have websites with additional information and resources. For more information, please visit our website at http://www.llewellyn.com.